Light Rail in

Michael Taplin

Capital Transport

First published 1995

ISBN 185414 180 5

Published by Capital Transport Publishing
38 Long Elmes, Harrow Weald, Middlesex

Printed by CS Graphics, Singapore

Contents

Introduction	4
Austria	8
Belgium	14
Bosnia-Hercegovina	19
Bulgaria	20
Croatia	21
Czech Republic	23
Finland	28
France	29
Germany	36
Hungary	84
Italy	88
Netherlands	94
Norway	98
Poland	100
Portugal	110
Romania	112
Slovakia	122
Spain	124
Sweden	126
Switzerland	129
Turkey	136
Yugoslavia	137
United Kingdom	138

Photographs in this book are by Mike Russell unless otherwise credited.

The front and back cover photographs (Bochum and Prague respectively) are by Karel Hoorn.

The photograph opposite (Berlin) is by Brian Hardy.

The photographs on the title page and back page (Strasbourg and Dusseldorf) are by Karel Hoorn.

Trams are the backbone of public transport in the Swedish city of Gothenburg. Two ASEA built units are seen in 1994. *Karel Hoorn*

Welcome to *Light Rail in Europe*, an illustrated introduction to the tramway and light rail systems serving Europe's towns and cities. Space and lack of data have prevented inclusion of those countries which were once part of the Soviet Union within our definition of Europe, but a total of 152 systems in all the other countries of Europe are represented. The aim is to give a brief description of each system with basic tabulated rolling stock details, and appropriate illustrations to give the reader a feel for the town or city. The author has visited all but ten of the systems (six in Romania) and is grateful to his colleagues in the Light Rail Transit Association for making up the difference.

The street tramway came to Europe from the USA, and electrification just before the turn of the century was a parallel trend in America and Europe. However the early development of private motoring and the industrial clout of the bus industry ensured that the tramway went in to a steep decline in North America before the Second World War, while in Europe only the smaller and hopelessly uneconomic systems disappeared at this time. The ravages of the European war might have been the excuse to follow the American trend: indeed it turned out to be so in Britain and France. Elsewhere the opportunity for reconstruction was also seen as the opportunity for further tramway development, with Germany leading the way. Thus when America 'rediscovered' light rail in the 1980s, it turned to Germany for its technology and rolling stock. Similarly the introduction of light rail in British cities has been based on continental practice and licensed or imported rolling stock. How different from the French approach where the investment in new and rejuvenated systems has largely stayed within France.

The latest design on the Brussels system, supplied by BN between 1993 and 1995.
Colin Stannard

Post-war trends on modern systems have been to upgrade track for higher speeds, and to segregate it from other traffic where possible, thus increasing the commercial speed, and improving the attractiveness to passengers and economics of operation. In Germany, and to some extent Belgium, subways for tram lines in the central area were seen to be necessary: an expensive solution which could be financed when times were good but caused progress to slow dramatically when recession arrived. However many see tram subways as ducking the issue of restricting the motor car in the city centres, and argue that hiding the tram away and making the stops difficult to reach can have a negative effect on patronage. Cities such as Gothenberg in Sweden, and Basel and Zürich in Switzerland, demonstrate the success of the alternative approach: keep the tram on the surface, visible and easily accessible, and keep the motorist under strict control to ensure that the surface trams can run nearly as fast as if they were in subways.

Rolling stock trends have been to larger cars and fewer staff, again improving the economics of operation. The three-car set of two-axle trams with a crew of four (driver plus three conductors) was replaced firstly by two-car sets of bogie trams, and then by the articulated car. Here Germany led the way, while Switzerland pioneered the implementation of self-service fare systems so that the remaining staff member (the driver) usually handles no cash or tickets. Such a system eliminates delays at stops, but requires a heavy investment in ticket machines at stops, and effective inspection plus on-the-spot fines to deter those who may be tempted to take a free ride. Also most systems will be trying to capture their regular passengers with long-term ride-at-will season tickets. The prices of these are often heavily subsidised by the municipality as part of its environmental programme to encourage public transport patronage. Again contrast this attitude with that for the new British systems, where one of the conditions for a government capital grant is that the revenue from fares must cover operating costs and earn a profit for the private sector.

If the commercial speed of a tramway has been maximised by segregation and taking fare collection away from the car, what else can be done to improve its attractiveness? The latest trend is to speed boarding and alighting times by eliminating the steps that passengers have to go up and down when boarding and alighting (and which discourage many less-mobile potential passengers). The easiest way (without breaking new ground on car design technology) is to have platforms at stops level with the car floor: the platforms can be accessed by ramps or lifts so that, for instance, mothers with pushchairs and wheelchair users can use the system without difficulty. For new systems this may be possible, particularly where the line is segregated away from the street: Utrecht – Nieuwegein is an example. However achieving this standard at all stops on an existing system would take years and be hugely expensive, even if it were physically possible. Only a few German cities, such as Hannover, are heading in this direction.

The answer is to lower the floor of the tram so that there can be level boarding from a low platform (or high kerb) at each stop. Trams have high floors because of the need to clear axles and motors in the power bogies. Modern technology can now address this problem by eliminating axles and fitting small but powerful motors in redesigned wheelsets. All the manufacturers started to address this problem from the mid-1980s, when it became clear that the low-floor tram would be the trend of the 1990s. Adding a low-floor centre section to an established design is relatively easy, but the benefits are confined to just a small part of the tram. Lowering the area between the power bogies was the next solution, giving a much greater low-floor area accessible through several doors, but still retaining steps within the car. However the holy grail of politicians, operators and manufacturers is the tram with a completely flat low floor. The first examples have entered service in the last year, and many hundreds are on order for systems across Europe. Unfortunately the rush to develop these cars has seen many different solutions developed, so that standardisation has been abandoned and prices have climbed accordingly.

So now we have tram services that are fully accessible by everyone in the community: not just new and pioneering systems such as Grenoble, but also completely re-equipped and rebuilt systems such as Lille. And how about bringing regional rail services right into the high street instead of terminating at a relatively inconvenient railway station, leaving passengers to change for the last part of their journey. Karlsruhe in Germany has shown that this is possible with light rail, developing a dual-voltage car that can run quite happily at 20 km/h in a pedestrian precinct and at 100 km/h on the main line, sharing track with Inter City expresses. A few strategic track links, with suitable voltage-changeover arrangements between the two systems have opened up a range of possibilities which are likely to be copied by several other systems. And the response from the public has been patronage increases of up to 300 per cent. If you want to take an inspirational European tour that will show you the best of the latest developments in four countries, your itinerary should run something like this: Sheffield, Manchester, Lille, Strasbourg, Karlsruhe, Freiburg, Basel, Lausanne, Geneva, Grenoble, Paris, Nantes.

Most systems have a rich history, and are traditional tramways that have been upgraded to light rail standards to a greater or lesser extent. An increasing trend of the last 10 years is the construction of completely new systems, often in cities where the tram disappeared as an old-fashioned relic many years ago. These state of the art systems provide an inspiration to all those looking for an effective means of preventing the motor car from destroying their city, and it is pleasing that British cities are now joining this trend. The more readers who bring the message home from the European mainland about what can be done, the better.

Controversy continues about the use of the term light rail to describe upgraded tramways. In truth it is difficult to find a cut-off point between tramway, light rail and metro, since systems exist at every point in the spectrum representing a gradual convergence from one type of system to another. If this book had been called Tramways in Europe, it would have been difficult to justify the inclusion of systems such as Genoa and London's Docklands Light Railway. We hope that readers can leave the semantics behind and discover the reality for themselves.

Travelling through Europe, individually or in a group, has never been easier, and the introduction of through rail services from Britain to the continent in 1994 means that a system such as Brussels or Lille can become a day trip destination no different from Manchester or Sheffield to many people. Language difficulties may remain, but travel on continental tramways is usually assisted by ticket sales off the car and by the availability of ride-at-will tickets for one day or 24 hours. We hope this book will encourage more people to find out for themselves.

Photography in the public domain should represent no problem, even in eastern Europe, although the position in the former Yugoslavia is unclear at the time of writing. Please seek permission before venturing on to private property such as depots: most operators are concerned about your health and safety rather than their own secrets!

In this book, each system is headed as follows:

Town or city name   *Opening year and track gauge*   *System size*

For towns and cities where anglicised spellings exist, these are used as they will be more familiar to most of our readers. In these cases the local spelling is given in brackets in the headings. The opening year is the year that the first tramway was opened, regardless of mode of traction or subsequent replacement of a narrow gauge system by a 'new' standard gauge one. The track gauge is expressed in millimetres: standard gauge is nominally 1435 mm, but small differences are found. The system size is the sum of the single measurement of each section of line (single or double track): official statistics often represent the sum of individual route lengths, which inflates the size of the system. In some countries data on system size is not available and has been estimated from scale maps (Poland and Romania in particular). We would be pleased to have any corrections.

The rolling stock data is not intended to represent a detailed fleet list. Only the main batches of cars in regular public service are shown, and the presentation of a complete series does not mean that the batch is complete. Many older cars, and individual new cars, will have been withdrawn. Odd cars kept for works or special duties and museum cars are not shown. Those requiring detailed fleet lists are referred to the bibliography in the appendix. Details shown are:

Fleet numbers   *Car type*   *Year built*   *Builder*

Car types: A = Articulated, M = Motor tram, B = Trailer, number = number of axles or wheel pairs.

Gloucester, June 1995   MICHAEL R. TAPLIN

AUSTRIA

Austria's four main cities all have tramway systems: that in the capital, Vienna, is the largest system described in this book. At the other end of the scale is the Gmunden "Toonerville Trolley" with a short line linking town and railway station. In many ways Austrian tramway practice follows German traditions, and most of the rolling stock has been built under licence from German manufacturers. However low-floor cars developed for Vienna have shown an independence of design. Austrian tram builders are Rotax (formerly Lohner, and now part of the Bombardier group) and Simmering-Graz-Pauker (SGP, recently acquired by the Siemens group). Upper Austria is a land of electric light railways, which show many tramway influences. The Salzburg local railway is likely to be upgraded and extended as a light rail transit link across the city.

Gmunden   1894   1000mm   2.5 km

The beautiful lakeside town of Gmunden is built on a hillside with the Federal Railways station at the top of the hill and the lakeside promenade at the bottom. The short tramway connects the railway station with the town centre over a mixture of street track and private right-of-way, and provides connections to and from all trains. The maximum gradient of 9.6% makes it one of the steepest adhesion lines in Europe. Off-peak service requires only one tram, but a second is required at peaks, and a third bogie car is in reserve. Two of these trams are second-hand from the Vestische system in Germany. A 1912 museum tram sees occasional use. The tramway is operated by the light railway group Stern & Hafferl and has been threatened with closure because of increasing motor traffic in the central area: however an effective retention campaign has been fought by local people, and the tramway may be re-extended to Rathausplatz. The Stern & Hafferl electric light railway from Vorchdorf-Eggenberg has its terminus at Gmunden Seebahnhof, by the lake across the bridge beyond the tram terminus.

Rolling stock
5	M2	1912	Graz	
8	M4	1962	Lohner	
9-10	M4	1952	Duewag	Ex-Vestische

Graz   1878   1435mm   30.3 km

Graz is an industrial city in southern Austria, but has a well-preserved city centre with a tram/pedestrian precinct. Pro public transport policies have seen an increasing importance given to the six-route municipal tramway system, with enhanced frequencies, tramway extensions (starting with route 6 at St Peter) and a new depôt. A new cross-river route is proposed, and the central tramway junction of Jakominiplatz (served by all routes) is being completely rebuilt with a new track layout and turning circle. The tram fleet has been modernised, with some new cars, and second-hand articulated trams from Duisburg and Wuppertal in Germany. The 1986 SGP cars may be rebuilt with low-floor centre sections; earlier articulated trams are already receiving conventional centre sections. Most sections of route are on street track, but route 1 includes private right-of-way over the former light railway to Maria Trost. A tramway museum exists at the latter terminus and preserved cars give public rides on summer Sundays.

Rolling stock

261-283	AM6	1963-6	Lohner/SGP	
501-510	AM8	1978	SGP	
521-537	AM8	1973	Duewag	Ex-Duisburg
551-571	AM8	1954-60	Duewag	Ex-Wuppertal
581-	AM8	1963-6	Lohner/SGP	With ex-Wuppertal centre sections
601-612	AM6	1986/7	SGP	

Facing page Gmunden 5 climbs through the town past the office building of Stern & Hafferl.
Below Jakominiplatz is the hub of the Graz tramway system.

The Innsbruck trams are dominated by the surrounding mountains and the tramway system is busy with both residents and tourists.

Innsbruck   1891   1000mm   36 km

This picturesque Tirolean city is built in the river valley between mountains at the crossroads of rail and road routes. There are two urban tram routes, a steeply-graded suburban line (route 6) to the mountain resort of Igls (all municipal), and the nominally-independent (but operationally-integrated) Stubaitalbahn light railway running 21 km south to Fulpmes on private right-of-way. This operates from the main railway station over the tram tracks, including a one-way street loop around the central area. After some uncertainty about the future role of the tramway (following the introduction of trolleybuses), the system has been modernised with a new depôt and articulated trams, including second-hand examples from Bielefeld and Hagen in Germany (with double-ended rebuilds on the Stubaitalbahn). Some older stock is preserved in a museum at Berg Isel, and sees occasional use on tourist services. It is planned to extend the system to new park-and-ride sites on the outskirts of the city.

Rolling stock

31-43	AM6	1957-63	Duewag	Ex-Bielefeld
51-52	AM8	1963	Duewag	Ex-Bielefeld
71-77	AM6	1966/7	Lohner	
81-88	AM8	1960/1	Duewag	Ex-Hagen, Stubaitalbahn

Linz 1880 900 mm 15.3 km

The industrial and commercial centre of Upper Austria, Linz is an expanding city with an attractive central area. A main tram route 1 links the southern and northern suburbs (the latter including 5 km of express tramway opened in 1977), with a second route 3 branching to the main railway station, and serving Urfahr station on the north bank of the river Danube. Street track in the pedestrianised city centre is followed by reservation in the suburbs. The municipal system has been modernised in recent years with new articulated trams, including rather unusual 10-axle variants. A further extension to the southern suburb of Ebelsberg is planned and consideration is being given to a regional light rail system. Part of the former electric light railway from Ebelsberg to Sankt Florian remains as a weekend museum operation. The Stern & Hafferl Linzer Lokalbahn is a modernised electric light railway with its terminus near the main railway station. At Urfahr tram terminus is the base station of the Pöstlingbergbahn, an adhesion mountain railway with 10.6% gradients operated by the municipal transport undertaking, and featuring tramway-type rolling stock with trolley pole current collection, including the original cross-bench cars for summer weekend service.

Rolling stock

41-56	AM10	1984-6	Rotax
61-67	AM8	1970/1	Lohner
68-79	AM10	1977	Rotax
81-88	AM8	1970-2	Lohner

A 10-axle articulated tram passes through the centre of Linz.

Vienna (Wien)   1865   1435 mm   188 km

The Austrian capital has a mixture of old and new suburbs surrounding the historic centre. It is served by the largest European tramway system outside Russia. Although this has been contracting as the metro system expands, suburban extensions are still under construction. The system is mostly street track, with reservation in newer suburbs, and private right-of-way on the line south-west to Rodaun. Trams cross the river Danube to Floridsdorf, with feeder lines from other northern suburbs. In the centre some trams run around the historic Ring, with others terminating at adjacent interchanges. There is a tram subway on the southern part of the outer ring. Rolling stock modernisation has brought a large fleet of articulated trams. The Stadtbahn light rail transit line serving the western outer ring is being extended north across the river to Floridsdorf, and south to take over the tramway to Siebenhirten in April 1995. It uses tramway-style rolling stock, including new low-floor cars. As well as the three-line metro (U-Bahn), there is also an S-Bahn local rail service provided by the Federal Railways. A large tramway museum exists at Erdberg depôt, and preserved trams often run sightseeing tours around the city.

Rolling stock

1	AM6	1995	SGP	Low floor
102-159	M4	1955-7	SGP	
601	AM8	1995	SGP	Low floor
701-748	AM4	1961-4	SGP	
1001-1090	B4	1954-9	Lohner	
1101-1290	B4	1960-2	Lohner	
1301-1373	B4	1974-7	Rotax	
1401-1488	B4	1977-87	Rotax	
1502-1588	B4	1955-59	SGP	
1901-1930	B6	1979-83	Rotax	Stadtbahn
2601-2668	AM6	1992-4	Rotax	Stadtbahn
4001-4078	AM6	1977-87	SGP	
4301-4315	AM6	1977-87	Rotax	
4401-4459	AM6	1959-66	Lohner	
4461-4524	AM6	1967-73	Lohner	
4525-4560	AM6	1973-5	Rotax	
4601-4630	AM6	1961/2	SGP	
4631-4868	AM6	1966-76	SGP	
4901-4945	AM6	1979-85	Rotax	Stadtbahn

Below
The articulated tram plus trailer set is the standard operation in Vienna.

Vienna (Wien) - Baden (WLB)   1435 mm   30.4 km

This interurban tramway runs over street track and through the Vienna tram subway to a terminus at Ring-Oper in the city centre, and on reserved track and private right-of-way to the spa town of Baden via picturesque wine villages south of the city. There is a tram every 15 minutes at peak periods, with multiple-unit operation south of Wolfganggasse depôt in Vienna. The modern fleet of articulated trams has completely replaced older stock, though there are some preserved examples of pre-war cars which appear on special service from time-to-time. There is some limited goods traffic to premises along the line, and a track connection to the Federal Railways.

Rolling stock
101-118   AM8   1979-93 SGP

A coupled set of WLB interurban trams crosses the railway bridge at Meidling arriving in Vienna from Baden. *M R Taplin*

Other lines

Light railways in the Stern & Hafferl group are electrified and often use tramway-style rolling stock (mostly second-hand from other European systems). These lines are in Upper Austria:

       Linzer Lokalbahn (Linz - Eferding - Waizenkirchen) 1435mm
       Neumarkt - Waizenkirchen - Peuerbach 1435mm
       Gmunden - Vorchdorf-Eggenberg 1000mm
       Vorchdorf-Eggenberg - Lambach 1435 mm
       Lambach - Haag-im-Hausruck 1435 mm
       Vöcklamarkt - Attersee 1000mm

Running out of Salzburg is the 1435 mm Salzburger Lokalbahn, a modernised interurban serving the region to the north of the city, and which recently took over the Stern & Hafferl line from Bürmoos to Trimmelkam. A museum group has a tramway collection at Mariazell (terminus of the narrow-gauge electric railway from St Pölten) with a short operating line to Erlaufsee. Another group has a collection of museum trams at Europapark in Klagenfurt, and operates a horse tram at weekends in high summer.

BELGIUM

In addition to its many urban tramways, Belgium was once criss-crossed by the interurban and rural lines of the Vicinal organisation. However in the 1960s most of this network was converted to bus operation, as were the urban trams in Charleroi, Liège and Verviers. Today transport remains firmly in public ownership, with the regional organisations De Lijn in the Flemish-speaking west and north and TEC in the French-speaking south and east, and the bi-lingual STIB/MIVB for Brussels in the centre. De Lijn has inherited the urban tramways in Antwerpen and Gent, as well as the former Vicinal coastal tramway based on Ostend. The future lies firmly with the tram in all these places. The TEC inherited what materialised of a grandiose scheme for light rail based on Charleroi, and has been slow to decide where the future lies. The current administration in Brussels favours tramway expansion, though funding is now tight. Rolling stock has been Belgian-built by tradition, with the La Brugeoise company (now BN) acquiring the rights to the PCC car in western Europe, and only recently abandoning this technology. However EC tendering regulations have introduced a competitive element.

Different liveries in Antwerp show the transition from MIVA to De Lijn.

This Brussels eight-axle tram has just left the subway at Midi station.

Antwerp (Antwerpen)   1873   1000mm   57 km

This Flemish city built by the river Schelde has a beautiful city centre surrounded by old-established suburbs, with new development concentrated on the west bank of the river, linked by road, rail and tram tunnels. The tramway system is part of the regional De Lijn operating group and has benefited from considerable investment in recent years. Street track in the city centre (including some surviving sections of gutter running) is being slowly replaced by sections of tram subway, and new reservations are being created in the suburbs to upgrade the system to light rail standards. In 1991 a new tram subway under the river to the west-bank suburb of Linkeroever was built, connecting with new surface reservation, and with a large park-and-ride facility at the outer terminus. Routes running north-west from the city centre will be the next to benefit from subway alignment. The standardised fleet of PCC cars features regular operation of coupled cars, and the trams are undergoing a major refurbishment programme. It is expected that new low-floor trams will be acquired as the system expands, but in the meantime some second-hand cars may be acquired to cope with increasing traffic. There is a transport museum at Edegem in one of the old forts that used to defend Antwerp.

Rolling stock

7000-7060	M4	1960-2	La Brugeoise
7061-7100	M4	1966	La Brugeoise
7101-7125	M4	1969/70	La Brugeoise
7126-7165	M4	1974/5	BN

Brussels (Bruxelles/Brussel)   1869   1435mm   134 km

The Belgian capital is officially a bi-lingual city (French and Dutch), and includes a relatively compact city centre, with the new European quarter adjoining it to the east, and older suburbs to the south and west. The large tramway system was substantially modernised in the late 1950s and in the 1960s, with significant tram subway construction, but progress was then overshadowed by the creation of the metro system. Recent policy has been in favour of resuming tramway modernisation: extensions have been built and a new fleet of low-floor trams has just entered service on route 91-94. These are replacing the original PCCs, while articulated cars using PCC technology are being modernised. The north-south subway across the city centre is in subway, as is the eastern part of the outer ring. The former was extended to the south in 1993, with two new branches. Street track elsewhere is slowly being put on reservation. The long reserved-track routes to the east (Ban Eik and Tervuren) are the showpieces of the surface system, though a short extension to Stalle park-and-ride in the south was opened recently. The former Vicinal tram subway near the Heizel exhibition grounds in the north has been renovated to provide a new link for the city trams in 1994. Another extension, in the north-east, has taken tram tracks to a new workshop facility at Haren. There is an extensive tramway museum at Woluwe depôt on the line to Tervuren, and on summer weekends museum trams are in regular public service on surface tracks between Montgomery and Tervuren.

Rolling stock

2001-2051	AM6	1993-95	BN
7001-7049	M4	1951-3	La Brugeoise
7051-7155	M4	1955-58	La Brugeoise
7156-7171	M4	1970-1	La Brugeoise
7500	AM6	1962	La Brugeoise
7701-7827	AM6	1972-3	La Brugeoise
7901-7961	AM8	1977-8	BN

The Industrial landscape west of Charleroi provides the backdrop for a tram in Vicinal livery.

Charleroi   1887   1000mm   20 km

The old industrial and coal-mining area of Hainaut in the French-speaking region of Wallonie was once served by a network of urban and interurban tramways, mostly operated by the state-run regional tramway organisation known as the Vicinal. The majority of the lines in this area were replaced by bus operation in the 1960s and 1970s, and the region itself is in substantial decline as the traditional industrial base has withered away. As part of an attempt to rejuvenate the area rather grandiose plans for a light rail system to be developed out of the remaining tramway operation were approved, with much upgrading of surface tracks, subways in Charleroi and elevated alignments through outer suburbs. A new fleet of articulated trams was purchased. However progress has been dogged by political wrangling, and a conspicuous lack of success in achieving good results with the first sections to be built: now economic difficulties mean that some work carried out may not be brought into service. At present just two services are provided, linking Charleroi Sud railway station with Anderlues in the west (a mixture of surface, subway and elevated track) and Gilly to the east (almost all in subway). A second subway to the east remains disused, as do modernised surface tracks to Gosselies in the north (though part of this line is used for access to Jumet depôt). Work continues on the east side of the subway ring in central Charleroi. Less than half the fleet is used in service. A museum group operates Sunday summer services on part of the former network between Lobbes and Thuin (south of Anderlues).

Rolling stock

6100	AM6	1980	BN
6101-6154	AM6	1981	BN

A Gent tram, second-hand from Bochum, in the new regional transport authority livery. *Karel Hoorn*

Gent 1875 1000mm 30 km

This Flemish city in western Belgium is renowned for its architecture in the central area, and is surrounded by a mixture of old-established and new and expanding suburbs. The largely street-based tramway system has expanded with a new reserved track route to the north (Evergem) and another to the south-east (Melle), while work is in progress on new routes to the south, beyond the present terminus at Sint-Pieters railway station. Trams and pedestrians mingle in the narrow streets of the old city centre. The trams are operated by the regional transport authority De Lijn, and had a standardised fleet of double-ended PCC cars for maximum flexibility. Indeed the operation is renowned for its ability to keep tram services running despite route blockages caused by road works, using temporary crossovers for turn backs. The fleet will need to expand when the next extensions are opened, and pending delivery of new articulated low-floor cars, second-hand stock is being acquired from Bochum-Gelsenkirchen in Germany.

Rolling stock

01-46	M4	1971-2	La Brugeoise	
47-54	M4	1974	La Brugeoise	
60-69	AM6	1961-2	Duewag	Ex-Bochum

Ostend (Oostende)   1885   1000mm   55 km

An interurban tramway runs the whole length of the Belgian coast from De Panne in the west to Knokke in the east, centred on the port resort of Ostend. There is street track through Ostend, leading to a new tram and bus station outside the railway station. Street track is also found in some of the urban areas along the route, but most of the alignment is on reserved track or private right-of-way, permitting high-speed operation. The lines to the east and west are worked as a through service on most journeys. In the summer there are many short-workings, with up to eight trams/hour between the main resorts. Work is starting on an extension at the west end of the line from De Panne to Adinkerke railway station and there is a possibility that through operation over the railway line from there to Dunkirk in France is a future option. The modern articulated trams are a single-ended version of those used in Charleroi; 10 have been equipped with low-floor centre sections. A few older trams are used for special trips from time to time.

Rolling stock

6000	AM6	1980	BN	
6001-6049	AM6	1982	BN	6040-9 are AM8
6102	AM8	1981	BN	
6131	AM6	1981	BN	

The Belgian coastal tramway links Ostend with De Panne and Knokke.

Other Lines

At Han-sur-Lesse in the Ardennes a former Vicinal metre-gauge tramway survives as a commercial operation to provide a link for tourists between the village centre and the entrance to the famous underground caverns, as part of a round trip. This line was never electrified and is worked by diesel trams hauling open trailers. There is a museum of Vicinal trams at the former Schepdaal depôt west of Brussels. A regional transport museum including trams exists at Liège.

BOSNIA-HERCEGOVINA

This new state created from part of the former Yugoslavia has yet to enjoy the integrity of its frontiers, and the future is clearly dependent upon the form of any long-term peace agreement. In the meantime travel to the area is not advisable.

Sarajevo   1895   1435mm   16 km

The standard-gauge tramway was opened in 1960 to replace a narrow-gauge system and includes a street loop around the central area, plus a branch to the railway station, with a long interurban line running west to the suburb of Ilidza. This line has been extended on reserved track. Before the civil war second-hand Washington PCC cars were replaced by new Tatra trams. Tramway operation was suspended in 1992 due to the war, with the depôt, many trams and much track destroyed by shelling. However efforts to resume a token service were successful in March 1994, and it is hoped that a regular service can be built up using about 10 trams that can be made serviceable. The longer term future will depend upon the outcome of the conflict and the availability of aid for reconstruction. Some replacement Tatra trams are being donated from Czechoslovakia.

Rolling stock

201-290	AM4	1973-83	Tatra

An animated scene in Sarajevo before the conflict.

BULGARIA

This former Communist state has always been rather isolated, both economically and in terms of tourism. The capital city has the only tramway system, which is set to be retained and modernised, but a large-scale switch to electric traction in other urban areas has been achieved by the use of trolleybuses.

Sofia   1901   1009/1435mm   208 km

The Bulgarian capital is a large and expanding city with many new suburbs surrounding the older built-up area. The extensive tramway is the backbone of the city transport system operated by the municipality, although a metro has recently been opened. The central area features largely street track, but west of the railway station there is a complex of tram subways adjacent to a large depôt. The traditional interurban line to Knayezhevo in the south-west was built on reserved track, and many of the new extensions built in recent years are also on reserved track. There is an attractive private right-of-way through the woods to Pl. Zavera in the south. In the eastern suburbs the narrow-gauge tramway has been replaced by a new standard-gauge line from 1987, and this has now been extended in to the city centre. It is expected that a cross-city standard-gauge tramway will be created. The Sofia tramway has built the majority of its fleet in its own workshops throughout the post-war period, and developed its own design of articulated tram which has been produced in six and eight-axle variants. Experiments with a convertible-gauge version for use on the new standard-gauge line were not very successful, and the undertaking turned to Tatra for its second batch of standard-gauge trams. Tatra has subsequently delivered narrow-gauge trams as well. The economic turmoil associated with the abandonment of Communism has meant that future plans for new trams and gauge conversion have slowed down. Second hand Duewag trams are being acquired from Bonn.

Rolling stock

101-211	AM8	1973-80	Sofia	801-825	AM6	1985-6	Sofia
300	AM6	1976	Sofia	826-827	AM6	1990	Sofia
301-327	AM8	1977/8	Sofia	828-831	AM6	1987-8	Sofia
400-467	AM6	1979-85	Sofia	832-863	AM6	1990/1	Sofia
501-502	AM6	1985	Sofia	875-899	AM6	1969-71	Sofia
503-504	AM6	1988	Sofia	900	AM8	1991	Sofia
601-675	AM6	1968-71	Sofia	2001-2040	M4	1991	Tatra
701-725	AM6	1985	Sofia	4001-4031*	AM6	1986	Sofia
726-729	AM6	1986	Sofia	4101-4137*	M4	1989	Tatra
730-799	AM8	1971-3	Sofia	*Standard-gauge			

A Sofia articulated tram descends through the woods to Pl. Zavera. *M R Taplin*

CROATIA

The first outbreak of the 1990s conflict in the former Yugoslavia affected eastern Croatia, and the final border here is by no means clear. The major city of Zagreb, further west, is committed to its trams and can be visited without problem. The small system at Osijek is difficult to reach at present. The settlement of the Yugoslav conflict is an essential pre-requisite to future urban transport investment.

Zagreb   1891   1000mm   45 km

The Croatian capital has been physically unaffected by the war, but most development plans have been suspended because of the political and economic situation. Zagreb was an important regional centre of the Austro-Hungarian empire, and has architecture to match in the central area, though some new development has been superimposed. Recent growth has seen expanding suburbs, particularly south of the river Sava. The tramway system runs on street track in the city centre, with some gutter-running in the older suburbs. There has been significant expansion to keep pace with new development, and these lines are mostly on reserved track. A shuttle service on private right-of-way runs in to the hills to the north of the city. After a period of buying traditional rolling stock from Yugoslav builder Duro Dakovic, the undertaking switched to the purchase of Czech trams from CKD-Tatra. A prototype Duro Dakovic articulated car could not be followed by series production before the war intervened, but a local bus body-builder has now produced an articulated tram for trials.

Rolling stock

104-163	M2	1957-66	Duro Dakovic	
164-171	M2	1961	Duro Dakovic	Ex-Osijek
200	AM6	1965	Duro Dakovic	
201-230	M4	1974/5	Duro Dakovic	
301-350	AM4	1985/6	Tatra KT4	
401-430	M4	1976	Tatra T4	
431-485	M4	1979	Tatra T4	
486-494	M4	1983	Tatra T4	
591-700	B4	1954-66	Duro Dakovic	
701-730	B4	1974-5	Duro Dakovic	
731-741	B4	1969	Duro Dakovic	Ex-Belgrade
801-830	B4	1976	Tatra B4	
831-885	B4	1979	Tatra B4	
900	AM6	1990	Duro Dakovic	
901-913	AM6	1960-64	Duewag	Ex-Mannheim
2101	AM8	1994	Koncar	

In the hills above Zagreb a Duro Dakovic car is pictured on route 21.

The suburbs of Osijek show a Tatra tram on its roadside reservation.

Osijek   1884   1000mm   12 km

The town of Osijek saw fierce fighting during the early days of the Yugoslav conflict, and although now under UN ceasefire protection is still virtually surrounded by Serb forces. Tramway operation ceased during the fighting and trams and equipment were destroyed, but limited operation has since resumed. Due to the lack of information on the current position, the system is described as it was before the war. Osijek is an industrial town with a well-preserved city centre and straggling suburbs. The east-west tramway includes a large loop through the centre to serve the railway station. This is on street track: in the suburbs there is gutter-running street track and some reservation. The tram fleet was modernised by the import of modern cars from Czechoslovakia, including some Tatra trailers.

Rolling stock

6801-6810	M4	1968	Tatra T3
7211-7222	M4	1972	Tatra T3
8201-8204	B4	1982	Tatra B3
8223-8226	M4	1982	Tatra T3

CZECH REPUBLIC

The former Czechoslovakia was the hub of tramcar modernisation for Communist Eastern Europe, with its Tatra factory turning out some 1000 new cars each year, based on PCC licence. Since the demise of Communism and the introduction of market-based economies, sales outside the company's homeland have collapsed, and a large new factory stands idle apart from the construction of small batches for Czech and Slovak systems and some export orders. In these circumstances the recent association with the German AEG group came to nothing, but a large order has been secured from Prague. The larger Czech cities all have modern tramway systems in municipal ownership, and this tradition is likely to continue.

Brno   1884   1435mm   70 km

Brno is an important commercial and industrial city at the centre of the former Czechoslovakia, and is well-known for its trade fairs. Although many old buildings remain in the centre it is a modern city with expanding suburbs. The tramway system has always been at the forefront of developments and upgrading to light rail standards started in the 1960s. All extensions built since then have been on reserved track and built for 80 km/h operation. There is street track in the city centre, including a pedestrian precinct. A new route from the city centre to the south-west suburbs is under construction. Like all Czech cities, the fleet is standardised on Tatra trams, with the latest KT8 articulated cars working alongside a few T2 trams still in service. The first Tatra low-floor trams are on order. A large collection of museum trams from Czechoslovakian systems has been assembled at the former Lisen depôt in the eastern suburbs.

Rolling stock

1003-1006	AM6	1967	Tatra K2	
1018	AM6	1969	Tatra K2	
1023-1117	AM6	1973-77	Tatra K2	
1118-1132	AM6	1982/3	Tatra K2	
1405-1494	M4	1958-62	Tatra T2	
1495-1510	M4	1963	Tatra T3	
1511-1580	M4	1966-8	Tatra T3	
1589-1603	M4	1972	Tatra T3	
1604-1652	M4	1985-9	Tatra T3	
1701-1702	AM8	1986	Tatra KT8	
1703-1723	AM8	1989/90	Tatra KT8	
1724-1728	AM8	1993	Tatra KT8	Built for Volgograd, but diverted

Some of the last Tatra T2 trams remain in service in Brno.

Liberec   1897   1000mm   21 km

This small city in northern Bohemia lies in the formerly disputed territory of the Sudetenland. The compact city centre is built on a steep hill and its narrow streets have changed little over the years. A long tram route links the straggling suburbs, and operates through semi-rural scenery in places, with a mixture of street track and reservation. An interurban tramway built in 1955 connects Liberec with the adjacent town of Jablonec, running through fine scenery with much private right-of-way: however its future is threatened because Jablonec is unwilling to make a contribution towards the operating subsidy. Single-track sections with passing loops are found on both lines. Liberec plans to convert its main route to standard gauge in 1997, and many sections of three-rail track have already been laid in readiness for the changeover, with an ex-Prague tram obtained for trials. The tram fleet is standardised on Tatra T3 cars.

Rolling stock

35-48	M4	1973	Tatra T3
49-58	M4	1983	Tatra T3
59-81	M4	1986-7	Tatra T3

Most   1901   1435mm   19 km

This town in the most heavily-industrialised area of northern Bohemia has been completely relocated since 1975 due to the spread of open-cast coal mining, and the new town is south of the old. The modern tramway system was opened in 1957 (replacing a former metre-gauge system) and links Novy Most with the adjacent town of Litvinov. The tramway alignment has also been relocated several times. Most of the system is on reserved track or private right-of-way: there is some street track in Litvinov. Because of its light rail characteristics the system is often used for trials of new designs of Tatra tram. One T5 tram built as a demonstrator for Kalinin in the then USSR returned to Most and is still in use. More recently articulated trams have arrived to supplement the standard T3 cars.

Rolling stock

203-298	M4	1982-5	Tatra T3
273	M4	1976	Tatra T5
300-313	M4	1987	Tatra T3
315-322	AM8	1986-9	Tatra KT8

Left This Liberec Tatra T3 is on the interurban route to Jablonec.
Right A coupled set of Most trams runs through the streets of Litvinov.

This Olomouc T3 demonstrates the bright new livery now being introduced in place of the former red and cream.

The centre of Ostrava with a coupled set in a new livery.

A gutter-running track layout in Plzen is a typical survival from the days of the Austro-Hungarian empire.

Olomouc   1899   1435mm   14.2 km

This Moravian town has changed little over the years with many old buildings in the central area and a mixture of residential and industrial suburbs. The tramway system serves the main traffic arteries, mostly on street track, but with some reservation in suburban areas, including single track on the Neredin line. It is planned to build new routes to modern residential areas.

Rolling stock

126-133	M4	1967-8	Tatra T3
134-145	M4	1970	Tatra T3
146-184	M4	1983-7	Tatra T3

Ostrava   1894   1435mm   58 km

The industrial conurbation of northern Moravia is centred on Ostrava, and once included links with the Silesian industrial region in nearby Poland. Four transport undertakings merged by 1953 to form the municipal operation which has developed a standard-gauge tramway network to replace the former narrow-gauge lines (although those to Bohumin in the east of the area were replaced by buses). The modern system features a high degree of reservation or private right-of-way, including a long interurban route to the west that is single track with passing loops. There is some street track in the old centre of Ostrava. The former tramway goods traffic has now ceased and a fleet of Tatra trams serves industrial plants and modern residential areas.

Rolling stock

594-598	M4	1960/1	Tatra T2	Ex-Usti nad Labem
600-699	M4	1958-62	Tatra T2	
701-748	M4	1965-8	Tatra T3	
749-772	M4	1970-3	Tatra T3	
773-798	M4	1976	Tatra T3	
802-804	AM6	1966	Tatra K2	
805-809	AM6	1969	Tatra K2	
810-811	AM6	1983	Tatra K2	
901-1027	M4	1982-8	Tatra T3	
1101-1110	M4	1994	Tatra T6	
1500	AM8	1984	Tatra KT8	
1501-1515	AM8	1989	Tatra KT8	

Plzen   1899   1435mm   26 km

This is the industrial centre of western Bohemia, famous for brewing and the Skoda armaments plant. The city centre is quite well preserved, and surrounded by large modern residential districts. The tramway system has much expanded in recent years from the street tramway serving the central area by the addition of new lines, including much reserved track, to serve the new housing areas. Standard T3 trams have been supplemented by new articulated cars.

Rolling stock

101-106	M4	1963-4	Tatra T3	Ex-Prague
160-171	M4	1964-7	Tatra T3	
172	M4	1970	Tatra T3	
173-207	M4	1972-6	Tatra T3	
208-245	M4	1982-83	Tatra T3	
246-287	M4	1985-7	Tatra T3	
288-299	AM8	1989	Tatra KT8	

Prague (Praha)   1875   1435mm   125 km

The Czech capital is a beautiful city on the Vltava river with a well-preserved central area, and extensive suburbs for housing and industry, with much new development. Investment in the large tramway system was overshadowed by metro construction for many years, but new extensions continue to be built to light rail standards. The central network has thinned as the metro opened, but extensive sections of street track remain here and in the older suburbs. There are six bridges across the river that carry trams. The historic castle district on the hill west of the city centre is served by trams, including a tree-lined reservation: other routes to the north and west include some steep gradient sections built in recent years. A new line being built from Branik to Modrany in the south was due to open in May 1995. At one time the fleet comprised over 1000 standard T3 trams, but articulated cars have arrived in recent years, and traffic has fallen with increasing motorisation following the fall of Communism. 150 Tatra T6 trams are on order. A splendid tramway museum has been established at Stresovice depôt, and is open at weekends during the summer. Museum trams operate a city tour service during the summer months.

Rolling Stock

6102-6607	M4	1962-65	Tatra T3	
6608-6715	M4	1967/8	Tatra T3	
6716-6992	M4	1970-6	Tatra T3	
7001-7252	M4	1982-7	Tatra T3	
7253-7292	M4	1989	Tatra T3	
8005-8106	M4	1976-81	Tatra T3	Renumbered from earlier cars
9001-9004	AM8	1986	Tatra KT8	
9005-9048	AM8	1989-90	Tatra KT8	

The Prague fleet includes these KT8 eight-axle trams.

FINLAND

The relative isolation of Finland and its relationship with the former Soviet Union held back development for many years, and the tramway system in the city of Turku was converted to bus operation. However the larger Helsinki system has now been thoroughly modernised, with further expansion planned, and international tendering for low-floor trams is in progress. Previous trams have been built in Finland under German licence.

Helsinki   1891   1000mm   70 km

The Finnish capital on the Gulf of Bothnia is an attractive city where the shipyards lie over the hill from the city centre and the suburbs are green and spacious. The tramway system has grown with the city. There is street track in the older part of the city centre, and a reservation down the main thoroughfare Mannerheimintie. Most suburban lines are built on reserved track, including the new link through Pasila in the north. Circular route 3 provides an easy sightseeing tour around the city. The modern metro serves the eastern suburbs and has not affected the tramway system, apart from the creation of interchanges. It is planned to develop the tramway system further, with more extensions and new links in the city, while low-floor articulated trams are to be ordered. The fleet is a mixture of older bogie trams with trailers and more modern articulated cars, all built in Finland. A new tramway museum has been established in part of Töölö depôt.

Rolling stock

1-30	M4	1959	Karia/Valmet
31-70	AM6	1973-5	Valmet
71-112	AM6	1985-6	Valmet
331-375	M4	1955-6	Valmet
501-530	B4	1957-8	Karia

Delivered in red and grey, Helsinki 65 has now reverted to green and cream livery. *Ken Harris*

FRANCE

The decline in French urban public transport evident in the 1960s has been reversed thanks to a positive commitment to investment from successive governments, and this has been particularly evident in a renaissance of tramways. The existing systems at Lille, Marseille and St-Étienne have been modernised and new systems built in several cities, with more planned. However Bordeaux, Rennes and Toulouse have opted for the VAL mini-metro system, and plans for new tramways in Brest and Reims were thwarted by local issues. More recently both Bordeaux and Rennes have delayed their definitive choice of VAL. The new systems have led the way in making mainstream public transport fully accessible for disabled passengers, and display a very high standard of built design. The dominance of domestic manufacturer Alsthom has been upset by the effect of EC regulations on competitive tendering.

A Grenoble low-floor tram climbs from the subway under the railway. *M R Taplin*

Grenoble   1987   1435mm   14.6 km

The city lies in the shadow of the French Alps, and has a thriving centre with modern suburbs. The first line of the brand-new tramway system was opened in 1987 and set new standards for the creation of an effective surface route through an established city centre. The construction of the tramway was accompanied by widespread environmental improvements and pedestrianisation along the corridor served, linking western and southern suburbs. A second line has been built to the north-east to serve the University and more extensions are under construction, firstly south to Echirolles. Although street-based the tramway mixes with other traffic very little other than at intersections thanks to the comprehensive traffic management system. The University line includes its own bridge over the river Drac. The trams used are a stylish low-floor design (giving level boarding at all stops) and the system has succeeded in boosting public transport patronage in the city and reducing the number of journeys made by car, as well as bringing full accessibility to the core public transport system.

Rolling stock

2001-2020	AM6	1986-7	Alsthom
2021-2032	AM6	1989	Alsthom
2034-2036	AM6	1992-3	Alsthom

Lille   1874   1000mm   19 km

The industrial and commercial centre of northern France is the focus for the adjacent towns of Roubaix and Tourcoing close to the Belgian border. The urban trams were replaced by buses but the separate ELRT tramway (known locally as le Mongy) has survived as an interurban system linking the railway stations in Lille with Roubaix and Tourcoing, mostly using reserved track on the wide boulevards that were created at the turn of the century. The tramway has recently been upgraded to light rail standards, with new subways in Lille (interchange with the VAL mini-metro, and the new international rail station) and underpasses at major intersections along the route. Some street track remains alongside the canal basin at Tourcoing. A new depôt has been built to house a new fleet of Italian-built low-floor trams, which replaced the existing rolling stock (second-hand articulated trams from Germany) in May 1994, when the traction voltage was increased from 600 to 750 V dc. The Amitram group has a working museum line alongside the canal at Marquette-lez-Lille, north-west of Lille, with summer weekend operation.

Rolling stock

01-24	AM7	1993/4	Breda

Marseille   1876   1435mm   5.9 km

France's second city is a Mediterranean port and industrial centre, the home to a cosmopolitan population. A large tramway system was replaced by buses and trolleybuses, apart from one line, route 68, which entered the central area through a short subway. This has been retained and modernised with a section of street track beyond the subway leading to a private right-of-way to the outer terminus, a suburban bus interchange. The subway terminus has been remodelled as an interchange with the new metro. There are plans to extend the line further in the suburban direction. The fleet of PCC cars was boosted when the opening of the metro brought increased traffic to the line.

Rolling stock

2001-2016	M4	1968/9	La Brugeoise
2017-2019	M4	1984	BN

Lille introduced its low-floor trams into service on 6 May 1994 using an Italian design assembled locally. *M R Taplin*

A Marseille tram set kicks up the dust on the street track.

Nantes   1985   1435mm   26.7 km

Nantes is a modern city and port on the river Loire and was the first French city to re-introduce trams under the Government's pro-public transport initiative. The first line was opened in 1985, running east-west across the city to link suburbs (and bus interchanges) with the city centre. The line is entirely on reserved track: the eastern section including part of a railway alignment. In the city centre it runs along a wide boulevard beside the quays on the north bank of the river. A second line was opened in 1992, running south from the city centre on its own bridge across the river and then to the suburb of Rezé, where there is some street track (although motor vehicles are restricted to residents). This line has been extended to the north, reaching the University in 1993 and Orvault in summer 1994. The original fleet of high-floor two-section trams was extended with a long low-floor centre section in 1992, and new trams to this design have been delivered.

Rolling stock

301-320	AM8	1984/5	Alsthom
321-328	AM8	1988	Alsthom
329-334	AM8	1992	Alsthom
335-346	AM8	1993	Alsthom

Paris   1992   1435mm   9.1 km

The French city is served by a dense metro network, but outside the central area this has a radial pattern, as do nearly all the local rail lines. The operating authority RATP has found that passenger demand on some inter-suburban corridors is more than can be effectively handled by buses operating on the highway, and therefore is planning a reserved-track public transport outer ring. The section between St Denis (SNCF station) and Bobigny (metro) has been built as a street-based, but largely reserved track tramway (opened in 1992), also serving La Courneuve metro at the mid-point. There is street track in the historic centre of St Denis, but most motor vehicles are excluded. A second section of the outer ring is under construction as a tramway, starting at La Défense in the west, then running south and taking over the former SNCF line between Puteaux and Issy-Plaine, eventually continuing to Porte de Versailles. The first part of this section should open in 1996. RATP uses Grenoble-type low-floor trams. The main French museum tram collection is located at the former St Mandé depôt in the eastern suburbs.

Rolling stock

101-117	AM6	1991/2	Alsthom

Rouen   1994   1435mm   16.1 km

The historic city on the river Seine is building a two-route tramway. Public service was inaugurated on 17 December 1994, to Sotteville and Quevilly, while work continues from Sotteville to Universitaire. The completed system involves a subway under the central area (serving the railway station), running south to surface for a bridge across the Seine, then on two reserved-track lines to Grand Quevilly and Universitaire. Grenoble-type low-floor trams are used.

Rolling stock

101-128	AM6	1993/4	Alsthom

The Nantes cars
with low-floor
centre sections
are amongst the
longest trams in
service anywhere.
M R Taplin

Paris 101 departs
from the Hotel de
Ville stop in
Bobigny.

Rouen 114 leaves
the subway junc-
tion with the
Sotteville line at
Ave de Caen, en
route to Quevilly.
M R Taplin

St-Étienne   1881   1000mm   11.6 km

This industrial town near Lyon is built in a narrow valley and has retained tramway operation on the north-south trunk route which carries 80,000 passengers per day. Street track through the central area is largely segregated from motor traffic. Reserved-track extensions have been built at both north and south ends of the system: the line to the north, opened in 1991, includes a new depôt. The fleet of PCC trams built under licence from La Brugeoise was supplemented with five new articulated cars (one has been rebodied to a modern design). The fleet has now been modernised by the delivery of new articulated low-floor trams from Vevey/Alsthom, and a high-frequency service is provided. Trolley poles are still used for current collection.

Rolling stock

501-530	M4	1958/9	Ateliers de l'Est	
901-915	AM6	1991/2	Vevey/Alsthom	
951-955	AM6	1968	La Brugeoise	Ex 551-555

Strasbourg   1994   1435mm   12.6 km

The historic city beside the river Rhine, the regional centre of Alsace and home of the European Parliament, has built a tram line which inaugurated public service on 26 November 1994. The line starts in the north-west suburb of Hautepierre and runs on reserved track to a short subway which serves the railway station. The line continues south through the city centre on pedestrianised streets, then on reserved track to the southern suburb of Illkirch (initial terminus at Baggersee). The modern design of low-floor tram was built in Great Britain by ABB at York.

Rolling stock
1001-1026   AM8   1994   ABB

Facing page This St Étienne PCC is assured of a good load of passengers from Soleure terminus.

Below Strasbourg 1003 at Homme de Fer stop in the pedestrianised city centre. *M R Taplin*

GERMANY

The post-war modernisation of West German tramways set the standard that many other countries followed, and provided the basis for a strong industry that has since achieved much export success. Mass-production of articulated trams from 1957 and off-car ticket sales with one-man operation from the 1970s were two of the important milestones in improving efficiency. Progress in East Germany was much slower, but by the time of reunification many systems were equipped with Tatra trams, although trackwork left much to be desired. Huge sums are now being invested in bringing systems in the east up to western standards, and virtually all new trams are to low-floor designs. The Duewag company (now part of the Siemens group) has always led the way with tramcar development, though smaller builders have thrived on regional preferences. Many systems are expanding and new systems proposed for Erlangen, Hamburg, Oberhausen and Saarbrücken. The Karlsruhe system with through operation from regional railways to city tram tracks points the way to new developments in the second-half of the 1990s.

Below A simple central reservation provides priority for this Augsburg tram.
Facing page Three eras of rolling stock on the Kirnitzschtalbahn at Bad Schandau.

Augsburg　　1881　　1000mm　　25 km

The historic Bavarian city on the river Lech keeps most traffic out of its attractive old town, but the trams carry passengers right to the heart of the central area on street track. There are six routes to the more modern suburbs, including some reserved track on the longer lines to Göggingen and Haunstetten. The outer end of the Kriegshaber route is single track, but work is about to start on an extension beyond the terminus. For many years the tram fleet comprised entirely unusual five-axle trams (essentially a München-type three-axle car with a rear body section supported on a bogie), but after delivery of some conventional eight-axle trams and the acquisition of second-hand stock from Stuttgart, a new fleet of low-floor cars is planned, with a prototype in service.

Rolling stock

401-13/51-63	AM4	1961/2	Esslingen	Ex-Stuttgart
522-551	AM5	1956-64	MAN	
601	AM6	1993	MAN	Low floor
801-812	AM8	1976	MAN/Duewag	
8001-8012	AM8	1985	MAN/Duewag	

Bad Schandau　　1898　　1000mm　　8.1 km

Bad Schandau is a small town on the river Elbe south-east of Dresden and near the Czech border. The town is reached from its railway station by a ferry across the Elbe. The Kirnitzsch valley runs east from the town in to the area known as the Saxon Switzerland, to the renowned Lichtenhainer waterfall. A tourist tramway connects the town and waterfall. The line is single track with passing loops, and runs in the highway or on roadside reservation. An intensive service is provided during the tourist season, a less-frequent service during the winter. Two-axle trams of the standard type provide the basic service: more historic rolling stock supplements this at times of peak demand, and trailers are also used. The overhead power is supplemented by solar energy from panels in the depôt roof.

Rolling stock

1-2	M2	1957	Gotha	Ex-Plauen
4-7	M2	1938-44	Gotha	Ex-Dresden
21-24	B2	1963	Gotha	Ex-Leipzig

Berlin   1865   1435mm   176.2 km

The former (and future) German capital was reunited in 1990: the large tramway system lies entirely in the former East Berlin, although plans have been approved to extend the system gradually into West Berlin and work has started on the link to Osloer Str and Seestrasse. The system is almost two networks, with just one line linking the central area network with that based on the historic town of Köpenick. The central area network is mostly on reserved track through rebuilt areas, although there is some street track in older suburbs such as Pankow. Light rail standard lines run to the new housing areas in eastern suburbs such as Ahrensfelde and Biesdorf. The line to the north-west suburb of Rosenthal is single track. The Köpenick network includes more traditional street track and some semi-rural operation, including single track to Mahlsdorf and Friedrichshagen. Under DDR administration the large fleet of standard two-axle motor trams and trailers was being replaced by Tatra articulated cars and twin-sets, but the last of the older stock is being replaced by a fleet of low-floor trams. Many Tatras are receiving heavy refurbishment to prolong their life and introduce western standards of comfort and operation.

The new low-floor trams built for Berlin in 1995 replaced trams from the early 1960s. *Brian Hardy*

Rolling stock

1001-1120	AM6	1994-7	AEG	Low floor
3001-3018	M2	1969	RAW	
3050-3080	M2	1959-61	RAW	
3081-3096	M2	1961	Gotha	
3110-3301	M2	1962-8	RAW	
3400-3738	B2	1960-63	RAW	
3701-3738	B2	1969	RAW	
3904-3999	B4	1962/3	Gotha	
3805-3863	M4	1962/3	Gotha	
5001-5xxx	M4	1989-90	Tatra	Refurbished
6001-6xxx	AM4	1984-6	Tatra	Refurbished
7001-7xxx	AM4	1982-84	Tatra	Refurbished
8101-8218	M4	1988-90	Tatra	
8501-8559	B4	1989/90	Tatra	
9004-9774	AM4	1977-86	Tatra	
9853-9882	AM4	1987	Tatra	

RAW motor and trailer at Fürstenwalderdamm on the Berlin system. *Karel Hoorn*

Above A coupled two-car unit on the Bielefeld system at Subrackstrasse. *Brian Deans*
Facing page Duewag trams also form the entire fleet of the Bochum-Gelsenkirken system.
Karel Hoorn

Bielefeld   1900   1000mm   26.1 km

The modern town midway between the Ruhr and Hannover has received substantial investment to bring its metre-gauge tramway up to light rail standards, with tramway subways in the central area (serving the railway station) and reservation in the suburbs. New extensions have been built on private right-of-way to Schildesche and Milse, and a new line to the University is being built, but the outer end of the Babenhausen route is still single track. The entire fleet of first-generation Duewag articulated trams has been replaced by a standard fleet of Stadtbahn cars for the subway operation. These have been supplemented by a new single-ended design with doors on both sides.

Rolling stock

516-539	AM8	1982/3	Duewag
540-559	AM8	1986/7	Duewag
560-579	AM8	1994-5	Duewag

Bochum-Gelsenkirchen   1894   1000/1435mm   101.9 km

These two towns form part of the Ruhr conurbation and are served by one municipal transport undertaking which has two links with the metre-gauge Essen tramway to the west. The tramways are perhaps the most traditional of the Ruhr area in terms of layout and surroundings, with long routes, much street track and single-track sections on all lines. However there has also been modernisation, with high-speed sections on reservation and tram subways in the centres of Bochum and Gelsenkirchen. In Bochum the north-south route from Herne to Querenburg has been converted to a standard-gauge Stadtbahn, with the northern section entirely in subway since 1989. On the metre gauge, first-generation articulated trams are being replaced by new low-floor cars, while Stadtbahn route U35 is worked by standard-gauge Stadtbahn-B cars.

Rolling stock

33-53	AM6	1967-9	Duewag	
301-333	AM6	1976/7	Duewag	
334-355	AM6	1981/2	Duewag	
401-442	AM6	1992-4	Duewag	Low floor
6001-6013	AM6	1988/9	Duewag	Standard-gauge
6014-6025	AM6	1992/3	Duewag	Standard-gauge

Bonn   1891   1435mm   51.6 km

The Federal capital is served by two urban tram routes and interurban Stadtbahn lines to Köln, Siegburg, Bad Honnef and Bad Godesberg. The Stadtbahn lines are substantially modernised, running in subway in the central area to serve the railway station and with a subway approaching completion in Bad Godesberg. Elsewhere reserved track or private right-of-way is the norm, apart from the section beyond Königswinter on the Bad Honnef line. Service is provided by Stadtbahn-B cars. On the urban tramways, which do not use the subway (but do serve the station), and include much street track, the rolling stock of the late 1950s has been replaced by new low-floor cars. An extension has been built in the northern suburb of Rheindorf. Two Rhein bridges are crossed by trams. The two routes to Köln are jointly-operated with that undertaking.

Rolling stock

201-214	M4	1957-60	Duewag	Sold to Sofia, Bulgaria
231-240	AM6	1959-60	Duewag	Sold to Sofia, Bulgaria
281-285	B4	1962	Duewag	Sold to Sofia, Bulgaria
286-289	B4	1967	Duewag	Sold to Sofia, Bulgaria
7351	AM6	1973	Duewag	Stadtbahn
7451-7467	AM6	1974/5	Duewag	Stadtbahn
7571-7578	AM6	1975	Duewag	Stadtbahn
7651-7654	AM6	1976	Duewag	Stadtbahn
7751-7760	AM6	1977/8	Duewag	Stadtbahn
8371-8378	AM6	1983	Duewag	Stadtbahn
8451-8456/71	AM6	1984	Duewag	Stadtbahn
9351-64/71-6	AM6	1993	Duewag	Stadtbahn
9451-9474	AM6	1994	Duewag	Low floor

The standard Stadtbahn-B car is in service on Bonn's longer routes.

A new alignment in Brandenburg, but served by the typical two-axle set from DDR times.

Brandenburg   1897   1000mm   19.6 km

This town is built on the river Havel west of Berlin, and as with many urban centres in the former DDR, is recovering rapidly from its rather run-down appearance, but does boast much traditional architecture. The tramway runs from the railway station on a large street-track loop through the centre, with suburban extensions, including a recent reserved-track line to the northern suburb of Hohenstücken. Running west through pleasant countryside is a long line to the large village of Plaue, single-track with passing loops: this line has been under threat of bus substitution, but seems to have been reprieved. Replacement of the fleet of standard two-axle trams and trailers by Tatra articulated cars had started, but future deliveries will be low-floor trams to western standards. A solitary second-hand articulated tram donated by Bielefeld in the early days of reunification sees little use.

Rolling stock

105-110	M2	1958-60	Gotha	
111-140	M2	1961-6	Gotha	Ex-Chemnitz, Erfurt, Gera, Halle and Plauen
150-168	M2	1967-68	Tatra	
170-185	AM4	1979-83	Tatra	
208-43	B2	1958	Gotha	Also 250/3/70/1/5
244-280	B2	1968/9	Tatra	Ex-Gera and Halle
284-299	B2	1957-62	Gotha	Ex-Gera, Plauen and Halle
804	AM8	1963	Duewag	Ex-Bielefeld

Brunswick (Braunschweig)　　　1879　　　1100mm　　　31.7 km

This expanding city east of Hannover has an historic and pedestrianised central area ringed by tramways. The tramway system has been extended and upgraded for a period of 30 years and bears little resemblance to its former layout. It is now mostly on reservation with extensions to modern housing areas such as Rühme, Broitzem and Heidberg, and more under construction. Only the routes to Volksmarode and Helmstedter Str have a more traditional aspect. The municipal undertaking has often bought trams from the nearby factory of Linke-Hofmann-Busch, and these designs differ from the standard Duewag look that is also represented in the fleet. Trailer operation is a feature of the system. Twelve low-floor trams are about to be delivered from LHB/AEG.

Rolling stock

6263-6267	AM6	1962	Duewag
6951-6956	AM6	1968/9	LHB
7351-7358	AM6	1972/3	Duewag
7471-7476	B4	1974	Duewag
7551-7556	AM6	1975	Duewag
7751-7762	AM6	1977	LHB
7771-7776	B4	1977	LHB
8151-8165	AM6	1980/1	LHB
8171-8182	B4	1981	LHB
8471-8472	B4	1984	LHB

This two-axle set in Brunswick carries a special livery for private-hire duties. The normal livery is white with orange trim.

Bremen   1876   1435mm   56.4 km

The north-German city on the river Weser features an historic and attractive city centre served by tram and pedestrian precincts, with industrial riverside suburbs and newer housing areas away from the river. Although the inner suburbs feature street track, outer sections have been upgraded to light rail standards on reservation or private right-of-way, especially the lines to Osterholz, Arsten and Huchting. A programme of route extensions has been delayed for financial reasons (but should now start), but money has been found to start replacing the unusual design of first-generation articulated trams and trailers by the latest type of low-floor tram. Two river bridges are crossed by trams.

Rolling stock

601-619	AB4	1959-62	Hansa	
620-643	AB4	1966-8	Hansa	
644-648	AB4	1968	Hansa	Ex-Bremerhaven
701-757	AB4	1973-6	Wegmann	Stadtbahn
801	AM6	1989	MAN	
3001-3078	AM8	1993-5	MAN	
3420-3444	AM4	1963	Hansa	
3445-3474	AM4	1967/8	Hansa	
3475-3479	AM4	1968	Hansa	Ex-Bremerhaven
3501-3559	AM4	1973-6	Wegmann	Stadtbahn
3560/1	AM6	1976/7	Wegmann	Stadtbahn

A Bremen Stadtbahn set on the elevated section of the Arsten line.

Chemnitz   1880   1435mm   22.3 km

In DDR times this industrial city was known as Karl-Marx-Stadt, and starting in 1960 had its decrepit narrow-gauge tramway replaced by a standard-gauge system featuring largely new alignments (the last narrow-gauge service closed in 1988). These new lines are mostly on reserved track, with four routes serving new housing areas focusing on the rebuilt city centre, and a link to the railway station. Further extensions are under construction. The fleet of Tatra trams is being heavily refurbished to western standards, but the first of a new generation, the low-floor ABB Variotram, is now in trial service.

Rolling stock

401-496	M4	1968-78	Tatra	
497-504	M4	1981-3	Tatra	
505-532	B4	1988	Tatra	
601	AM8	1993	ABB Waggon Union	Low floor
701-748	B4	1973-8	Tatra	
749/50	B4	1978	Tatra	
751-762	B4	1988	Tatra	

Cottbus   1903   1000mm   22.8 km

This attractive small town near the Polish border uses trams as the backbone of its public transport system, but the suburban lines to Ströbitz, Madlow and Schmellwitz feature awkward layouts and single-track sections that have created operating difficulties as motorisation has increased. New extensions, such as that to Neu-Schmellwitz, are on reserved track, as are some rebuilt sections in the central area, where there are two parallel routes. All operations are in the hands of a fleet of Tatra four-axle articulated trams, some of which have been refurbished to western standards. Others have been sold to Schöneiche.

Rolling stock

1-8	AM4	1978/9	Tatra	
9	AM4	1985	Tatra	Ex-Berlin
10-65	AM4	1979-90	Tatra	
66-72	AM4	1990	Tatra	Ex-Erfurt.

Darmstadt   1886   1000mm   36.2 km

Although a relatively small town, Darmstadt south of Frankfurt-am-Main is served by tram routes that extend well beyond the city-centre local services to link with adjacent communities such as Arheiligen, Griesheim and Alsbach. These flat and relatively straight lines permit the operation of some limited stop services which offer reduced running times. There is some street track (single track at Griesheim), but much central or roadside reservation. The short urban routes include a link to the railway station and a very traditional street tramway to Lichtenbergschule. The last west German undertaking to operate two-axle trams in regular service, fleet modernisation has been completed by the delivery of Berlin-built articulated cars, and by an order for low-floor trailers.

Rolling stock

21-33	AM6	1961/2	DWM	
91-97	AM6	1963	DWM	
151-162	B4	1965	Duewag	
171-178	B4	1954-60	Duewag	Ex-Bielefeld
7601-7608	AM6	1976/7	Waggon Union	
8209-8214	AM6	1982	Waggon Union	
9115-9124	AM6	1990/1	Waggon Union	
9425-9454	B4	1994/5	LHB	Low floor

Top A three-car Tatra
set on one of the latest
extensions in
Chemnitz. *Karel Hoorn*

Above A coupled
KT4D set passes a
mixture of architecture
in Cottbus.

Left Darmstadt's long
route to Alsbach
includes sections of
street track through
the villages.

Dessau   1894   1435mm   10.1 km

An industrial town with few features likely to attract visitors, Dessau has a tram route running south from the railway station through the city centre to the southern suburbs, with a new reserved-track branch to Kreuzbergstrasse. The street track has been mostly relaid after years of neglect, to coincide with the arrival from Duisburg of second-hand articulated trams that have replaced the former standard two-axle rolling stock completely. There are plans to take over a local rail line to operate an integrated service with the tramway.

Rolling stock

001-014	AM8	1964-66	Duewag

Below Ex-Duisburg articulated trams await entry into service in Dessau.
Facing page The Dortmund system still includes sections of single-track on the roadside.

Dortmund   1881   1435mm   73.3 km

At the eastern end of the Ruhr conurbation, Dortmund has a modern city centre and industrial suburbs. The long tram routes extend beyond these to modern housing areas and include a new light rail line to Grevel. More traditional routes to Brambauer and Wickede include single track with passing loops. Tram subways have been built for the north-west/south-east axis across the city centre (serving the railway station) and these feature dual-height platforms for operation by a mixture of standard trams and Stadtbahn-B cars. Some first-generation articulated trams remain in service. Further subways are under construction on the north-east/south-west axis. The University in the south-west suburbs, accessed by S-Bahn train, features the H-Bahn suspended monorail line.

Rolling stock

1-15	AM8	1974	Duewag	
85-91	AM8	1969	Duewag	
101-154	AM8	1978-82	Duewag	
301-354	AM6	1986-94	Duewag	Stadtbahn

Dresden   1872   1450mm   132.4 km

The capital of Saxony suffered terribly during the war, and has little pre-war architecture in the city centre, although some historic buildings have been reconstructed. The river Elbe is crossed by four bridges on the large tramway system, whose rolling stock was completely replaced in DDR times by Tatra T4 trams. After taking a few T6 cars, the first low-floor trams are on order for the system. The city centre layout features significant reservation on rebuilt sections. Much track reconstruction is going on, but most suburban lines still run in the street. The long routes along the north bank of the Elbe to Weinböhla and Bühlau may be susceptible to bus replacement, but extensions are under construction to new housing areas in the western suburbs. Outer sections of longer routes, to Weinböhla, Hellerau, Weixdorf, Kleinzschachwitz and Niedersedlitz feature single-line street track. The first low-floor trams have been ordered. Across the river bridge from Schillerplatz are two hillside lines: a cable tramway and a suspended cable monorail.

Rolling stock

222 014-048	M4	1970	Tatra	251 201	B4	1972	Tatra
222 101-138	M4	1971	Tatra	272 004	B4	1974	Tatra
222 161-178	M4	1981	Tatra	272 101-165	B4	1971	Tatra
222 202-250	M4	1972	Tatra	272 201-237	B4	1972/3	Tatra
222 301-364	M4	1973-83	Tatra	272 302-325	B4	1973	Tatra
222 401-484	M4	1974-84	Tatra	272 401-470	B4	1974-84	Tatra
222 501-559	M4	1975	Tatra	272 501-529	B4	1975	Tatra
222 601-648	M4	1976	Tatra	272 601-638	B4	1976	Tatra
222 701-720	M4	1977	Tatra	272 802-820	B4	1978	Tatra
222 801-870	M4	1978/9	Tatra	273 001-004	B4	1976	Tatra
222 913-998	M4	1969	Tatra	274 001-055	B4	1972-6	Tatra (refurbished)
224 001-072	M4	1972-77	Tatra (refurbished)	276 001/2	B4	1985-8	Tatra B6
226 001-004	M4	1985-8	Tatra T6				

Dresden trams now carry the city colours: this Tatra set is passing the historic Zwinger.

Düsseldorf   1876   1435mm   146.1 km

A modern city beside the river Rhein, Düsseldorf has retained a dense network of tram routes. Although there has been much modernisation of layouts, and subways have been built in the central area, much of the inner suburban operation features traditional street running using the large fleet of first-generation Duewag articulated trams. Trams cross the Rhein on two bridges to form a loop link with the nearby town of Neuss, although the authorities there are planning to exclude trams from their central precinct. Interurban light rail lines, using trams with buffet sections, provide high-speed services to the more distant towns of Krefeld and Duisburg, starting from the tram subway at the railway station. Longer urban routes run to Ratingen in the north and Benrath in the south. A new extension has been built to serve the University, south of the central area. There are sections of one-way working in parallel streets in the city centre. In addition to the older trams, the fleet includes 100 Düsseldorf-design cars of the 1970s, and more modern Stadtbahn-B cars. The first low-floor trams have been ordered.

Rolling stock

1205-1207	B4	1966	Duewag	2851-2867	AM8	1961	Duewag
1629-1631	B4	1955	Duewag	2964-2968†	AM8	1965	Duewag
1633-1700	B4	1960/1	Duewag	3037-3065	AM8	1974/5	Duewag
2301-2320	AM6	1956-8	Duewag	3101-3104	AM8	1975	Duewag
2351-2358	AM8	1958/9	Duewag	3201-3236	AM8	1974	Duewag
2401-2433	AM6	1956-61	Duewag	4001-4012	AM6	1981	Duewag
2451-2458	AM8	1958/9	Duewag	4101-4104‡	AM6	1988	Duewag
2497-2499	AM8	1960/1	Duewag	4201-4269	AM6	1985-8	Duewag
2501-2520	AM6	1956-8	Duewag	4270-4288	AM6	1992/3	Duewag
2551-2559	AM8	1958/9	Duewag				
2651-2673	AM8	1968/9	Duewag	†2966-8 ex-Neuss			
2751-2763	AM8	1965	Duewag	‡Buffet section			

Probably the most comfortable trams in Germany are these Düsseldorf cars from the mid-1970s.

Duisburg   1881   1435mm   61.4 km

North of Düsseldorf, and linked to it by an interurban light rail line, Duisburg is at the western end of the Ruhr conurbation and has a modern city centre with industrial suburbs. The long tram routes all serve the city centre subway (including the railway station) before surfacing to use a mixture of reservation and more traditional street track, reaching as far as Dinslaken in the north and Mülheim in the east (where there is dual-gauge track with the metre-gauge local tram system). A standard fleet of Stadtbahn-type articulated cars, to a design unique to Duisburg, operates all routes except the Düsseldorf interurban (which uses standard Stadtbahn-B cars).

Rolling stock

1001-1045	AM8	1986-93	Duewag	
4701-4714	AM6	1983/4	Duewag	Stadtbahn-B
4715-4718	AM6	1984/5	Duewag	Buffet section

Erfurt   1883   1000mm   29.3 km

The small city of Erfurt, with its well-preserved city centre, is served by what was one of the DDR's most progressive tramway systems. The original rather small street-based network was expanded north, west and south-east to new housing areas with segregated tracks on reservation or private right of way. The heart of the city is now attractively pedestrianised, with tram access maintained. The expansion is being continued. All older trams were replaced with Tatra KT4 cars, now being refurbished. An initial order for low-floor trams was delivered in 1994.

Rolling stock

401-444	AM4	1976-8	Tatra
445-493	AM4	1981-3	Tatra
494-553	AM4	1986-90	Tatra
601-604	AM6	1994	Duewag

Left Duisburg's own design of eight-axle car amongst typical industrial scenery.
Right The historic centre of Erfurt provides the backdrop to this busy scene, with one of the city's last batch of Tatra sets in the foreground.

Essen   1893   1000/1435mm   73.7 km

This city at the heart of the Ruhr suffered greatly in the war, but has been rebuilt in modern style. It is an important commercial and industrial centre, and its tramways link with the adjacent Mülheim and Bochum-Gelsenkirchen systems. Tram subway construction started in the 1960s and the central area network is complete: work continues on extensions to the north. Upgrading of lines to the west and south-west as part of the standard-gauge Ruhr Stadtbahn (opened from 1977) has taken place, and the subway from the railway station south is dual gauge. At Porscheplatz guided duobuses share the tram subway. Outer sections of route include more traditional street track. After some debate the metre-gauge tramways are to be retained, and fleet modernisation is being carried out with standard Duewag cars. The standard-gauge lines feature the Stadtbahn-B car, now being reinforced by rebuilt former Docklands Light Railway cars from London.

Rolling stock

1001-1020	AM8	1975/6	Duewag	
1101-1116	AM8	1979/80	Duewag	
1151-1166	AM8	1980-2	Duewag	
1171-1180	AM8	1982/3	Duewag	
1401-1415	AM8	1989/90	Duewag	
1751-1759	AM8	1962/3	Duewag	
1851-1863	AM8	1960-6	Duewag	
5101-5111	AM6	1976	Duewag	Standard gauge
5121-5128	AM6	1978	Duewag	Standard gauge
5141-5145	AM6	1985	Duewag	Standard gauge
5201-5211	AM6	1986	LHB	Standard-gauge, ex-DLR

The traditional tram routes in Essen are worked by these metre-gauge Stadtbahn cars.

Frankfurt/Main   1872   1435 mm   121.4 km

The commercial centre of the Federal Republic, Frankfurt is a modern city on the river Main. The large tramway system has been upgraded in a significant way, with a network of tram subways that were supposed to replace surface operation in the central area. However a policy change has seen the retention of the through route across the old city, and a stub terminus for lines from the north. The north-south subway is marketed as an U-Bahn, but is worked by Duewag U2-type Stadtbahn cars: suburban extensions, including the interurban lines to Oberursel and Bad Homburg are segregated. Tram routes have modern rolling stock (with low-floor trams being introduced), but include many sections of street track. There is private right-of-way on lines to Neu-Isenburg and Schwannheim in the south: the latter terminus features a tramway museum in former depôt buildings. More sections of tram subway are under construction. Two river bridges carry trams. Most of the 1956/7 trams have been donated to Bucuresti.

Rolling stock

001-016	AM6	1993/4	Duewag	Low floor
204-241	M4	1956-7	Duewag	
303-347	AM6	1968-71	Duewag	Stadtbahn
348-399	AM6	1975-8	Duewag	Stadtbahn
400-406	AM6	1984/5	Duewag	Stadtbahn
451-477	AM6	1979/80	Duewag	Stadtbahn
501-518	AM6	1995	Duewag	Stadtbahn
600	AM6	1963	Duewag	
601-645	AM6	1959-63	Duewag	
651-716	AM8	1972/3	Duewag	
717-750	AM8	1977/8	Duewag	
801-830	AM8	1963	Duewag	
901-908	AM8	1969	Duewag	
1204-1242	B4	1956/7	Duewag	
1801-1826	B4	1959-66	Duewag	

Frankfurt/Oder   1898   1000mm   25.1 km

The other Frankfurt is a small town on the Polish border, with the bridge forming the border crossing. After a period of stagnation, the town has extended its tramway system to new housing areas such as Markendorf and Neuberesinchen, nearly doubling its size. These lines are on reservation, but there is street track in the central area and older suburbs. Tatra KT4 trams were delivered towards the end of DDR administration, but standard two-axle motors and trailers are still in use until replaced by the recent order for low-floor trams.

Rolling stock

22	M2	1968	Tatra	Ex- Halle
14, 27-35	M2	1957-61	Gotha	Some ex-Gotha, Halle and Plauen
41-42	M2	1967/8	Tatra	Ex-Gera and Plauen
49	M2	1964	Gotha	Ex-Plauen
54/59	M2	1957/8	Gotha	Ex-Erfurt
103	B2	1967	Gotha	
112/114-121	B2	1972-4	RAW	
122	B2	1957	Gotha	Ex-Gera
134	B2	1967	Gotha	Ex-Plauen
127-131/138	B2	1957-61	Gotha	Ex-Halle and Erfurt
142	B2	1969	Gotha	Ex-Gera
201-234	AM4	1987-90	Tatra	
301-308	AM6	1994/5	AEG	

The street tramway in the old town of Frankfurt/Main has been retained despite closure plans.

Tram 303 is a new AEG low-floor tram for Frankfurt/Oder, and was loaned to Cottbus in 1995 for the Federal Garden Show. *T Schindler*

Freiburg/Breisgau   1901   1000mm   20.1 km

The historic and attractive city between the Rhein and the Black Forest has a determined environmental policy and the tramway system has been and is being extended to new suburbs. The trams operate through the narrow pedestrianised streets of the city centre (and through the old city gate towers of Martinstor and Schwabentor) and on routes to the north, south, east and west. The new construction has been to the west: Landwasser in 1989, with a new viaduct over the railway station, and in 1994 Weingarten. Double-ended trams are needed for the north-south route, which has stub termini at the attractive suburbs of Zähringen and Günterstal. Older four-axle articulated trams are being replaced by new stock with low-floor sections.

Rolling stock

115-122	AM4	1967-8	Rastatt	
201-204	AM8	1971	Duewag	
205-214	AM8	1981/2	Duewag	
221-231	AM8	1990	Duewag	Low floor centre sections
241-266	AM8	1993/4	Duewag	Low floor

The attractive city of Freiburg-im-Breisgau with four-axle articulated trams.

Gera 1892 1000mm 14 km

This attractive Vogtland town built in a long valley has one basic tram route (which has been extended north to Bieblach Ost and south to Zeulsdorf, with a short branch at the southern end to Zwötzen). The new extensions are on reservation; elsewhere there is street track. Unusually trams do not serve the railway station, which is 500m from the main street. The fleet of two-axle trams has been completely replaced in commercial service by Tatra KT4 cars.

Rolling stock

310-310	AM4	1978-81	Tatra	
311, 347	AM4	1979-81	Tatra	Ex-Brandenburg
312-344	AM4	1982-8	Tatra	
345/346	AM4	1979	Tatra	Ex-Berlin
348-363	AM4	1990	Tatra	

Görlitz 1882 1000mm 13.4 km

Another town on the eastern border of Germany, Görlitz is served by a traditional tramway system featuring a mixture of street track in the central area and single-track with passing loops in the suburbs, where there is some reservation. A reversing triangle is in use at Landeskrone terminus and there is another at Postplatz in the city centre. A small fleet of Tatra KT4 trams is in service, but most routes will use standard two-axle motors and trailers until second-hand trams from Mannheim arrive.

Rolling stock

001-011	AM4	1983-90	Tatra	
012-016	AM4	1988	Tatra	Ex-Erfurt
8	M2	1960	Gotha	
67	B2	1958	Gotha	Ex-Halle

Left The smart Gera livery sits well on the Tatra KT4D trams.
Right Tenements in Görlitz dwarf the single articulated car on route 1.

Gotha   1894   1000mm   25.3 km

The historic Thüringen town has one short urban tram route (street track) linking the two railway stations, and a long rural tramway out to forest villages and tourist spots (the Thüringerwaldbahn). This is largely on reservation or private right-of-way, single track with passing loops, and runs to Tabarz, with a branch to Waltershausen normally served by a shuttle tram. Although the fleet includes two-axle trams, and some of the few remaining four-axle two-rooms-and-a-bath trams in Germany, services on the Thüringerwaldbahn are operated by Tatra KT4 trams or second-hand Duewag articulated cars from Mannheim. Bochum is supplying second-hand trams for the urban routes.

Rolling stock

34-37	M2	1967/8	Tatra	
38/39	M2	1955	Gotha	
43-47	M2	1956-63	Gotha	
70-76	B2	1967-9	Gotha	
77-98	B2	1956-60	Gotha	Some ex-Frankfurt/Oder
201-216	AM4	1965-7	Gotha	
301-306	AM4	1981/2	Tatra	
320x443	AM6	1962-7	Duewag	Ex-Mannheim (9 cars)

Halberstadt   1897   1000mm   8.3 km

This well-preserved small town has decided to retain its tramway system against consultants' advice, and has built a short extension to a western suburb. A large loop runs around the central area, with branches to the railway station, Klusberge (a single-track shuttle) and Friedhof/Vogtei. The latter is a historic area where sympathetic reconstruction has just been completed. Two-axle trams are being replaced by second-hand refurbished four-axle articulated cars.

Rolling stock

30	M2	1966	Gotha	Ex-Halle
26-29/35	M2	1970-5	RAW	
35-41	M2	1956-61	Gotha	
46	M2	1966	Gotha	Ex-Cottbus
51-56	B2	1970-3	RAW	
60	B2	1960	Gotha	
61/66	B2	1965-9	Gotha	Some ex-Cottbus
151-160	AM4	1967	Esslingen	Ex-Stuttgart
161-163	AM4	1962-67	Esslingen	Ex-Freiburg

Halle   1882   1000mm   77.1 km

An industrial city on the river Saale, Halle has a dense network of urban tram routes (it was the largest metre-gauge tramway in the former DDR), mostly on street track, but with reservation on extensions to new housing areas such as Böllberg and Beesen. Running south is a long interurban tramway to industrial areas such as Leuna and Bad Dürrenberg, and the satellite town of Merseburg. A standard fleet of Tatra T4 trams has been supplemented by ex-Stuttgart articulated cars: both types are now being refurbished, while a small number of low-floor trams are appearing.

Rolling stock

101	B4	1967	Tatra	Ex-Belgrade
102-224	B4	1971-86	Tatra	
500/501	AM6	1992/3	Duewag	Low floor
851-890	AM4	1962-5	Esslingen	Ex-Stuttgart
901-902	M4	1969	Tatra	
904-1223	M4	1971-86	Tatra	

A new paint job and refurbished stop show the changes being wrought in eastern Germany, in this view of a Tatra tram on the Gotha system.

Delightful restoration and smart second-hand trams can be seen in Halberstadt.

Refurbished Tatra trams in Halle carry this smart livery.

Hannover   1872   1435mm   97.8 km

A rebuilt city renowned for its trade fairs, Hannover attempted a road system designed to cope with motor traffic in the central area, but then had to develop the most modern tramway/Stadtbahn system in Germany. All but one of the routes across the central area has been put in subway, and these are being extended in to the suburbs. In outer suburbs new extensions are being built on reservation and there is traditional street track only on the one route still worked by conventional trams (Empelde - Nackenberg via the Hauptbahnhof and Zoo). Other routes worked by Stadtbahn cars are slowly being upgraded with high-platform stops. An interurban line runs south-east to the nearby town of Sarstedt. A new Stadtbahn line will be built to serve the extended Fair grounds in the south-west, and a new generation of Stadtbahn cars has been ordered from LHB. A substantial collection of museum trams has been assembled at a site in Wehmingen, south of Hannover, with operation on summer Sundays and holidays.

Rolling stock

501-522	AM6	1961/2	Duewag
1501-1520	B4	1961/2	Duewag
6001-6100	AM8	1974-8	Duewag
6101-6260	AM8	1979-93	Duewag

Heidelberg   1885   1000mm   19.7 km

The historic university and tourist city on the river Neckar is linked with the Mannheim tramways by the OEG interurban, which includes a Heidelberg local service on its north arm to Handschuhsheim. Other routes are long suburban lines running from a central loop, including single-track sections at their outer ends. There is much street track, with reservation in rebuilt areas.

Rolling stock

201-204	AM8	1975	Duewag	
214-229	AM6	1964-8	Duewag	
230-244	AM6	1973	Duewag	
251-258	AM8	1985/6	Duewag	
261-272	AM6	1994/5	Duewag	Low floor

Jena   1901   1000mm   12.4 km

This rather nondescript manufacturing town south of Erfurt is served by a north-south tram route, largely on street track, with single track in the central area and to the north (Zwätzen). The line climbs a long hill to the southern terminus of Winzerla. A short single-track line running to Jena-Ost has been under threat of closure, but seems likely to survive. There are ambitious plans for extensions to south-east suburbs. The whole fleet is made up of two-axle standard trams, but a low-floor fleet is on order.

Rolling stock

101-118	M2	1957-61	Gotha	Some ex-Görlitz
132-139	M2	1971-3	RAW	
141/145	M2	1964/5	Gotha	
142-144/149	M2	1968	Tatra	
147/8	M2	1964/5	Gotha	
151-167	B2	1959-61	Gotha	Some ex-Gera and Görlitz
173-189	B2	1970-5	RAW	Some ex-Brandebburg and Görlitz
182/190	B2	1950-60	Gotha	Ex-Görlitz
191-195/198/199	B2	1964-9	Gotha	Some ex-Gera
196/197	B2	1968	Tatra	Ex-Halle

Top A modern Hannover car in Thielenplatz.
Westbury Marketing

Above Most trams in Heidelberg carry all-over advertising livery.

Left Scenes such as this view in Jena are fast disappearing from eastern Germany.

Karlsruhe 1877 1435 mm 94.2 km

Although rebuilt after war damage, the city has retained its traditional central street pattern focused on the palace of Prinz Karl-Wilhelm. The main shopping street is an extensive tram and pedestrian precinct served by most city tram routes and the interurban Albtalbahn, which runs long lines north to Hochstetten (partly on shared DB goods track) and south into the Black Forest (Ittersbach and Bad Herrenalb). The tramway is one of the most progressive in Germany, with suburban extensions featuring grassed reservations and bold plans for a regional network using dual-voltage trams running on the tramway and DB electrified lines. The first link has been created in the eastern suburb of Durlach to provide a local service on the railway to Gölshausen Bretten, and this has been so successful that other local lines are following in quick succession (Bruchsal, Wörth, Pforzheim and Rastatt). The dual-voltage cars are a modular development of the Stadtbahn design used on the Albtalbahn and some urban services. Older articulated trams are due to be replaced by low-floor cars. Eventually a tram subway will be built in the central area for regional services.

Rolling stock

101-107	AM8	1958/9	Duewag	
108-115	AM8	1959	Rastatt	
116-121	AM8	1966-9	Duewag	
122-125	AM8	1975	Waggon Union	
142-172	AM6	1959-64	DWM	
174-199	AM8	1964-9	DWM	
200-215	AM8	1972-8	Waggon Union	
501-520	AM6	1983-4	Waggon Union	
521-530	AM6	1987	Duewag	
801-836	AM8	1991-95	Duewag	Dual-voltage
851-880	AM8	1989-92	Duewag	

Kassel 1877 1435 mm 40.4 km

The modern centre of Kassel beside the river Fulda is noted for its adjacent Aue park, while a long straight highway with tramway reservation leads from the Rathaus west to the historic suburb of Wilhelmshöhe with its castle and hilltop Herkules monument. The Hbf railway station in the city centre, served by a short tram subway, has declined in importance with the opening of a new station at Wilhelmshöhe, served by the ICE high-speed trains. Older suburbs are served by street tramway routes, while new lines to Helleböhn and Altenbauna are on reservation or private right of way. Cross-river routes to Wolfsanger and Lindenberg include single-track sections. A mixed fleet of articulated cars features some trailer operation, and new deliveries of low-floor trams.

Rolling stock

301-317	AM6	1966-70	Wegmann	
358-366	AM6	1971	Wegmann	
401-416	AM8	1981	Duewag	
417-422	AM8	1986	Duewag	
451-475	AM6	1990-94	Duewag	Low floor
561-571	B4	1967-71	Credé	
576	B4	1956	Duewag	Ex-Frankfurt

The main street of Karlsruhe is a tram and pedestrian precinct.

Kassel trams are mostly double-ended to cope with the stub termini.

Cologne (Köln)   1877   1435 mm   142.2 km

Cologne on the river Rhein is dominated by its cathedral, but today is a modern city with extensive suburbs. The large tramway system has been continuously modernised: north-south routes in the central area are in subway, and these have been extended to the northern and western suburbs, while there are more subways in the east-bank suburb of Deutz. Surface lines are mostly on reservation (viaduct in the case of the northern ring) and are being upgraded with high-platform stops for the large fleet of Stadtbahn cars. A new fleet of low-floor trams is on order for the east-west surface routes: these will continue the replacement of the first-generation articulated cars (many now run at Konya, Turkey). There are four Rhine bridges carrying trams. The interurban light rail system, formerly the independent Cologne-Bonner Eisenbahn, provides links to Bonn by two routes.

Rolling stock

2001-2054	AM6	1973-8	Duewag		2301-2333	AM6	1995	Duewag
2095-2099	AM6	1977	Duewag		3001-3039	AM8	1968/9	Duewag
2101-2122	AM6	1984/5	Duewag		3101-3139	AM8	1969-71	Duewag
2192-2199	AM6	1985	Duewag		3211-3226	AM8	1968/9	Duewag
2201-2240	AM6	1987-92	Duewag		3701-3778	AM8	1963-9	Duewag
2251-2260	AM6	1987-90	Waggon Union		3801-3883	AM8	1964-66	Duewag

Krefeld   1883   1000mm   37.3 km

This modern industrial town north-west of Düsseldorf is linked to the latter by the Rheinbahn standard-gauge light rail line, but has its own expanding network of metre-gauge tramways which run on street track in the central area (resulting in some dual gauge track) and to eastern suburbs such as Uerdingen and Rheinhafen. Extensions to Elfrath and TEW are on reservation. A fleet of standard Duewag articulated trams is operated. Further extensions are planned.

Rolling stock

809-810	AM8	1964	Duewag
811-830	AM8	1972-6	Duewag
831-850	AM8	1980/1	Duewag

Leipzig   1872   1458mm   160.5 km

The important commercial and industrial centre of eastern Germany is a large city with a very extensive tramway system, mostly on street track, but with some newer lines, and the city centre ring, on reservation. The outer ends of long suburban routes to Taucha, Markleeberg, Knautkleeberg and Böhlitz-Ehrenberg feature single-track operation. The railway station is the largest in Germany and is served by the majority of tram routes. A standard fleet of Tatra T4 trams has been built up, and some are being refurbished to western standards, while the first low-floor cars are now being delivered.

Rolling stock

483-485	B2	1959	Gotha	Ex-Berlin
503-773	B4	1968-87	Tatra	
801-814	B4	1988-91	Tatra	
921-992	B2	1963-9	Gotha	
1001-1028	M4	1988-91	Tatra	
1144-1217	AM4	1964-7	Gotha	
1332/1334	M2	1959/60	Gotha	Ex-Berlin and Dresden
1501-1535	AM6	1995	Duewag	Low floor
1601/1602	M4	1970	Tatra	Ex-Dresden
1603-2197	M4	1968-86	Tatra	

Cologne keeps some Stadtbahn cars in special livery for services to the Messe exhibitions.
J M Bromley

Two cars of the batch delivered in 1980/1 are seen at Hauptbahnhof, Krefeld.
Westbury Marketing

The new blue and cream livery is carried by these Leipzig Tatra T6 trams.

Ludwigshafen   1878   1000mm   46.5 km

An industrial town on the river Rhein, Ludwigshafen is linked by two bridges to adjacent Mannheim, and both these carry shared tram routes. Tramways in the central area run in subway or pedestrianised streets, while suburban lines have been mostly rebuilt on reservation. Street track is found in Rheingönheim and Oggersheim. The town centre tramways are used by the nominally-independent Rhein-Haardt-Bahn (RHB), a light rail line linking Mannheim/Ludwigshafen with villages and towns to the west, ending in the sausage and wine town of Bad Durkheim. Outside the built-up areas this runs on private right-of-way. Its fleet includes articulated trailers and the long 12-axle articulated trams. The Ludwigshafen fleet is of standard six and eight-axle cars, but low-floor trams to a novel design are being delivered (including a seven-section version for the RHB).

Rolling stock

101-147	AM6	1959-67	Duewag	
148-159	AM8	1967-71	Duewag	
201-216	AM6	1995	Duewag low floor	
1012-1018	AM6	1960/3	Duewag	RHB
1019-1022	AM12	1967	Duewag	RHB
1031-33	AM8	1995	Duewag low floor	RHB
1051-1058	AB6	1960-3	Duewag	RHB
1123/1124	AM6	1959	Duewag	RHB
1217/1218	AB6	1959	Duewag	RHB

Magdeburg   1877   1435mm   55.7 km

This is a modern industrial city half way between Hannover and Berlin. The tramway system has a up to date layout, although there is plenty of street track in the suburbs. New lines to Olvenstedt, Barleber See and Neustadter See are on reservation. There are two bridges carrying trams across the river Elbe. A long interurban route runs south-east to Westerhüsen. A standard fleet of Tatra T4 trams is operated, but low-floor cars are now being delivered

Rolling stock

1001-1274	M4	1968-86	Tatra
1275-1286	M4	1989	Tatra
1301-1320	AM8	1995	LHB
2002-2141	B4	1969-86	Tatra
2143-2148	B4	1989	Tatra

Mainz   1883   1000mm   21.6 km

An historic city by the Rhein, Mainz has a pedestrianised city centre that is skirted by the tramway system, which is still mostly on street track. Long routes west to Finthen and south to Hechtsheim each have short new branches on reservation at their outer ends. The other routes, to Ingelheimer Aue and Bretzenheim feature single track on the outer sections. The replacement of first-generation articulated trams by low-floor cars is about to start, and there are ambitious plans to double the size of the system by building new routes.

Rolling stock

221-227	AM6	1958-61	Westwaggon	
229-235	AM6	1965	Duewag	
236-245	AM6	1960/1	Duewag	Ex-Heidelberg
271-276	AM8	1984	Duewag	
277-280	AM8	1976	Duewag	Ex-Bielefeld

Ludwigshafen's first articulated tram is still at work after 35 years service.

Magdeburg was a DDR system that managed to avoid painting its trams red and cream.

Mainz route 8 serves the industrial area close to the river Rhein.

Mannheim 1878 1000mm 47.2 km

Mannheim is a modern commercial city with a grid street layout in the central area that is crossed by tram/pedestrian precincts. The heart of the system, Paradeplatz, features co-ordinated departures at times when frequencies are reduced in the evening and on Sundays. Trams cross the Rhein to Ludwigshafen, and also on three bridges across the Neckar to northern suburbs. The layout of the system is mostly modern, with the outer end of the Vogelstang route to light rail standards on private right-of-way. Work is in progress on a new line to Neckarau in the south, and there will be large scale route alterations when this is opened in autumn 1995. The fleet of standard Duewag articulated cars is being replaced by low-floor trams to a common design with Ludwigshafen.

Rolling stock

318-320	AM6	1960	Duewag	Ex-Heidelberg
322-435	AM6	1960-4	Duewag	
436-450	AM6	1967	Duewag	
451-470	AM6	1970/1	Duewag	
501-523	AM8	1962-4	Duewag	Low-floor centre sections
601-650	AM6	1994-5	Duewag	Low floor

One of the latest low-floor trams on the Mannheim system at Kaiserring. *Karel Hoorn*

Mannheim - Heidelberg (OEG)   1887   1000mm   61 km

This interurban light railway, which started life as a steam tramway, links Mannheim railway station with the centre of Heidelberg by two lines, a direct route via Seckenheim, and a longer route via Weinheim. There is also a branch to Heddernheim, and this and the Weinheim - Heidelberg section are single track with passing loops. Street track or reservation is shared with the city systems at Mannheim or Heidelberg: elsewhere is mostly private right-of-way with some roadside reservation. Route integration with Mannheim is due in October 1995. A modern fleet of distinctive double-ended articulated cars is operated and the first low-floor cars have been ordered (the ABB Variotram).

Rolling stock

80-81	AM8	1960/1	Rastatt	
82-97	AM8	1966-9	Duewag	
98-110	AM8	1973/4	Duewag	
111-116	AM8	1988/9	Duewag	
191-205	B4	1962/3	Rastatt	
301-304	AM6	1962	Duewag	Ex-Bielefeld
311-314	B4	1962	Duewag	Ex-Bielefeld

The OEG interurban serves sections of street tramway.

A single bogie tram suffices for an evening departure in Mülheim/Ruhr.

Mülheim/Ruhr 1897 1000/1435mm 37.9 km

A modern town in the Ruhr conurbation, between Duisburg and Essen, Mülheim has a metre-gauge local system (including a through route to Essen via Borbeck) and standard-gauge lines to Essen and Duisburg. Essen, opened in 1977, is to Stadtbahn standards in subway or on viaduct; Duisburg has dual-gauge street track. The local routes are mostly street based, but a new extension to Möllhofstrasse is on reservation. There is a reversing triangle at Flughafen. The route to Landwehr is to be re-extended to the neighbouring town of Oberhausen. The well-kept tram fleet has been modernised with double-ended standard Duewag cars. Seven standard-gauge Stadtbahn cars work on the joint service to Essen. The first low-floor trams are on order.

Rolling stock

181-189	B4	1955/6	Duewag	
196-198	B4	1958	Duewag	
220-230	M4	1954/5	Duewag	
252-259	AM6	1958-60	Duewag	
260-262	AM6	1964	Duewag	
264	AM8	1958	Duewag	
271-276	AM8	1976	Duewag	
277-282	AM8	1977/8	Duewag	
283-290	AM6	1984-7	Duewag	
291-294	AM6	1992	Duewag	
5012-5016	AM6	1976	Duewag	Stadtbahn
5031-5032	AM6	1985	Duewag	Stadtbahn

The Munich three-axle tram sets are still a common sight in the Bavarian capital.

Munich (München)   1876   1435 mm   78.5 km

The capital of Bavaria is an historic city on the river Isar, with extensive suburbs. The development of the metro system has seen a substantial reduction in tramway services, and the undertaking planned to discontinue these. However political changes have seen the tramways come back into favour, and there are plans for new or re-opened lines. There is still much street track throughout the system, modern lines on reservation in the north and south-west having been abandoned in favour of the metro. A long interurban route runs south on private right-of-way to Grünwald. The unusual three-axle motor trams and trailers that were once the backbone of the fleet are now being withdrawn from service and many sent to Bucuresti. A new fleet of low-floor trams is being delivered.

Rolling stock

2003-2044	AM4	1966-8	Rathgeber	
2101-2170	AM8	1994-5	MAN	Low floor
2403-2457	M3	1956-9	Rathgeber	
2505-2535	M3	1963/4	Rathgeber	
2601-2620	M3	1964/5	Rathgeber	
2651-2670	M3	1965	Rathgeber	
2701-2703	AM6	1990/1	MAN	Low floor
3003-3040	AM4	1966/8	Rathgeber	
3402-3498	B3	1956-9	Rathgeber	
3501-3545	B3	1963/4	Rathgeber	

Naumburg   1892   1000mm   5.2 km

Operation of the single-track ring street tramway in this attractive small town between Leipzig and Erfurt has been suspended because of the poor state of the track, but local people are determined to see operation resumed and a limited tourist service on part of the line was provided in 1994 using two-axle trams on one section and a horse tram on another. More regular operation is planned to take place in future summers. In recent years the tramway ring service had been operated in one direction only.

Rolling stock

1	B2	1951	Werdau	Ex-Halberstadt
11-12	B2	1960-2	Gotha	Ex-Plauen
13	B2	1961	Gotha	Ex-Frankfurt/Oder
23-28	M2	1951-6	Gotha	Ex-Gera and Plauen
31-32	M2	1960	Gotha	Ex-Plauen
33-34	M2	1960	Gotha	Ex-Frankfurt/Oder
41	M2	1967	Tatra	Ex-Halle

Nordhausen   1900   1000mm   8.7 km

Another small town, at the south end of the Harzquerbahn steam-operated narrow-gauge railway, Nordhausen has been modernising its hilly three-route tramway and has built new extensions to the hospital (Kreiskrankenhaus) and Leimbach. The other route to Parkallee is single track with passing loops. There is a tram/pedestrian precinct along the main street leading to the station. Standard two-axle trams are being replaced by refurbished ex-Stuttgart and Freiburg four-axle articulated cars.

Rolling stock

40	M2	1957	Gotha	
59	M2	1965	Gotha	Ex-Leipzig
71-81	AM4	1959-62	Esslingen	Ex-Stuttgart

Nuremburg (Nürnberg)   1881   1435mm   39.8 km

Nuremburg fashions tend to follow those of Munich, so the future of the tramway system in this historic city was threatened by the investment in a two-line metro. However local pressure groups have succeeded in persuading politicians that the tramways have a future, so closures have stopped, extensions are planned and the first of a fleet of low-floor trams is on order. Extensions may be built, including a link to a new light rail system for the nearby town of Erlangen. In the meantime four-axle trams remain in more extensive use here than elsewhere in western Germany. The system is mostly street track, but the route to Bayernstrasse uses part of the subways built to provide rapid transit to the former rally grounds. A tramway museum is open at weekends in the former St Peter depôt.

Rolling stock

212-268	M4	1958-60	MAN	
301-356	AM6	1962-6	MAN	
361-372	AM8	1976/7	MAN/Duewag	Low-floor centre sections
1531-1610	B4	1959-66	MAN	

It remains to be seen if this scene in Naumburg has passed into history for ever, or whether efforts to revive the tramway will be successful.

Ex-Stuttgart articulated trams have brought much-needed modernisation to Nordhausen.

A Nuremburg tram set approaches track work in Allsberger Str.

Plauen   1894   1000mm   17.3 km

The compact tramway system in this attractive and hilly small town has been modernised in recent years and a new route built to Waldfrieden on reserved track. Elsewhere is mostly street track. Trams link both upper and lower railway stations via the triangular junction in the central area known as Tunnel (though this does not indicate any underground operation). With the construction of a turning circle at the Untere Bhf, the fleet has been standardised on single-ended Tatra KT4 articulated trams.

Rolling stock

201-235	AM4	1976-88	Tatra	
236-245	AM4	1987/8	Tatra	Ex-Zwickau

Potsdam   1880   1435mm   25.8 km

This historic city to the south-west of Berlin is linked to the latter by S-Bahn train service. The tramway system is the backbone of the public transport network, and a new extension has been built (Am Stern), using reserved tracks. However much of the system remains on street track, and there is single track with a reversing triangle at Kapellenberg terminus. The tram fleet has been standardised on Tatra KT4 cars: many of these are being heavily refurbished at present. Trolleybuses operated until suspended indefinitely in 1995.

Rolling stock

003-044	AM4	1977-83	Tatra	
045-0124	AM4	1985-7	Tatra	Ex-Berlin
100-1xx	AM4	1977-83	Tatra	Refurbished
200-2xx	AM4	1977-83	Tatra	Refurbished

Rostock   1881   1440mm   22.3 km

The modern seaport on the Baltic coast has greatly extended its tramway system in recent years, with new reserved track lines to the northern suburbs of Dierkow and Totenwinkel. Tracks are also on reservation in the rebuilt central area, but older suburbs have street track. Although a small batch of Tatras was acquired to start replacing the standard two-axle trams, most of the latter, and the two-rooms-and-a-bath articulated trams will go as new low-floor cars are delivered.

Rolling stock

601-622	M4	1988-90	Tatra	
651-700	AM6	1994/5	Duewag	Low floor
701-734	AM4	1961-5	Gotha	Some ex-Leipzig
755-789	M2	1958-67	Gotha	Some ex-Chemnitz, Magdeburg and Schwerin
791-793	M2	1971	RAW	
801-806	B4	1989	Tatra	
861-909	B2	1957-67	Gotha	
910/926/931	B2	1971-5	RAW	
911-950	B2	1965-9	Gotha	
951-962	B2	1970-5	RAW	

All-over advertising liveries such as this in Plauen have become common in eastern Germany.

Potsdam trams are now appearing in a distinctive new livery.

One of the last systems in the former German Democratic Republic to acquire Tatra trams was Rostock. This pair is approaching Hauptbahnhof.

Schöneiche - Rüdersdorf   1910   1000mm   15.2 km

This interurban tramway runs from Friedrichshagen S-Bahn station in the south-east suburbs of Berlin through the woods to the small town of Rüdersdorf. Although some track modernisation has been carried out, much of the line is single-track with passing loops. Once known for its fleet of individualistic self-built trams, the service is now run with second-hand Tatra KT4 articulated cars, though older trams remain in reserve.

Rolling stock

17-25	AM4	1981	Tatra	Ex-Cottbus
74-75	M2	1974/5	RAW	
77-78	M2	1960	Gotha	Ex-Cottbus
124	B2	1968	Tatra	Ex-Gorlitz
125-126	B2	1964-6	Gotha	Ex-Gorlitz

Single track on the Schöneiche tramway sometimes means a wait at passing loops.

Schwerin   1881   1435mm   22.2 km

Schwerin is a well-preserved lakeside medieval Mecklenburg town that is redis-covering tourism. However the modern tramway system is orientated towards large suburban housing areas, with new reserved-track lines to Pampow and Grosser Dreesch built to light rail standards in recent years. A single-track one-way loop operates around the central area. The fleet has been standardised on Tatra T3 (wider than the German-standard T4) trams and trailers, and these are going through a major refurbishment programme at present.

Rolling stock

201-293	M4	1973-81	Tatra	
301-358	B4	1973-83	Tatra	
359	B4	1988	Tatra	
401-418	M4	1983-88	Tatra	
1xx+2xx	M4	1973-83	Tatra	Refurbished

The single track loop through the centre of Schwerin links together reserved track suburban lines.

Strausberg   1893   1435mm   6.2 km

East of the Berlin city boundary, but served by the S-Bahn electric railway system, the Strausberg line links railway station and town centre on single track with passing loops, at first on private right-of-way through the woods, then on street track in the town. The service has operated using standard two-axle trams for several years, but ex-Kosice (Slovakia) eight-axle Tatra trams were imminent at the time we went to press in summer 1995.

Rolling stock

01-06	M2	1969	RAW	Ex-Berlin
001-004	B2	1969	RAW	Ex-Berlin

Left Off-peak service on the Strausberg tramway features a single Reko tram.

Right The hills of Stuttgart are exaggerated by this telephoto view of a metre-gauge set.

Stuttgart   1868   1000/1435mm   110.1 km

This attractive and hilly city, the capital of Baden-Württemburg, also has industrial areas alongside the river Neckar. The extensive tramway system has been partly regauged in recent years as part of an upgrading to Stadtbahn light rail standards (standard-gauge operation started in 1975), though with the construction of a network of central area subways this is marketed as the U-Bahn. Surface operation in the city centre is confined to the environs of Berliner Platz. Surface sections of standard-gauge lines are put on reservation where possible, and stops equipped with high-level platforms. There is a little standard-gauge street track (eg in Heslach), and rather more on the metre-gauge system. The lines south of Degerloch, to Vaihingen, Leinfelden, Möhringen and Plieningen were once part of the Filderbahn independent electric light railway, and include much private right-of-way. There is a rack tramway from Marienplatz to Degerloch. Many of the unusual metre-gauge four-axle articulated trams have been sold elsewhere as standard gauge Stadtbahn sets have been delivered. The museum tram collection is being moved in 1995 from Gerlingen to Zuffenhausen depôt.

Rolling stock

401-698	AM4	1960-4	Esslingen	Metre-gauge
3007-3104	M4	1985-88	Duewag	Stadtbahn
3105-3202	M4	1989-93	Duewag	Stadtbahn

Ulm   1897   1000mm   5.8 km

This historic and well-preserved small town in south Germany has a single surviving tram route served by a fleet of ex-Stuttgart four-axle articulated trams. The line is mostly street track, with some reservation near the railway station and private right-of-way at the eastern terminus Donauhalle. The local authorities wish to treble the size of the system by building routes to other suburbs.

Rolling stock

| 1-14 | AM4 | 1964 | Esslingen | Ex-Stuttgart |

Ulm purchased its GT4 trams from Stuttgart and initially adopted the same livery.

Woltersdorf   1913   1435mm   5.6 km

In south-east Berlin, one stop on the S-Bahn system from Friedrichshagen (Schöneiche tramway) is Rahnsdorf, also served by a Berlin tram route, This is the western terminus of an independent tramway to the village of Woltersdorf, another single-track line with passing loops. It begins on a private right-of-way and then runs in the street through the village. Second-hand standard two-axle cars are used.

Rolling stock

27-32	M2	1959-61	Gotha	Ex-Dessau, Dresden and Schwerin
88-92	B2	1960/1	Gotha	Ex-Schwerin

Woltersdorf livery is in a state of transition from cream, via orange, to blue.

Würzburg   1892   1000mm   19.4 km

Würzburg in northern Bavaria is a baroque architectural gem on the river Main and has expanded its small tramway system to increase the benefits of electric traction. The city centre streets served by the tramway are largely pedestrianised. There is street track on the routes to Zellerau, Grombühl and Sanderau. The long line to the southern suburb of Heidingsfeld features single track on the original route, and reserved track with steep gradients on the new route to Heuchelhof and Rottenbauer. A varied selection of first-generation articulated trams is to be replaced by a new low-floor fleet: cars with low-floor centre sections are already in service.

Rolling stock

201-214	AM8	1988/9	LHB	Low-floor centre sections
231-240	AM8	1967/8	Duewag	
241-248	AM8	1975	Duewag	
270-281	AM6	1962/3	Duewag	Ex-Hagen

Ex-Hagen articulated tram in scenic Würzburg.

Zwickau   1894   1000mm   9.1 km

This rather dull, industrial town near the Czech border has a two-route tramway system which until recently had seen little modernisation apart from delivery of some Tatra KT4 trams. Now the remaining two-axle cars are being swept away by a new fleet of low-floor articulated trams, and the largely street-track system has been extended with a new reserved track line to Eckersbach.

Rolling stock

901-912	AM6	1993/4	AEG MAN	Low floor
916/921	M2	1965	Gotha	Ex-Plauen
918-920/922-926	M2	1968	Tatra	Some ex-Halle
927	AM4	1983	Tatra	Ex-Plauen
928-949	AM4	1987-90	Tatra	
956/8	M2	1960	Gotha	
959-987/989-991	B2	1958-69	Gotha	Some ex-Halle, Leipzig and Plauen
988/992-999	B2	1967-9	Tatra	Some ex-Halle

Three-car sets of two-axle trams such as this in Zwickau are becoming a rare sight.

Other cities

Trams are set to return to the Ruhr city of Oberhausen in 1966 by northward extension of Mülheim routes. Plans are advanced for a light rail system based on Saarbrücken (and featuring Karlsruhe-style through running to local rail lines); also similarly for Erlangen (with a connection to nearby Nuremburg). The Hamburg senate has voted to re-introduce trams.

HUNGARY

The standard for Hungarian tramways has always been set by the large Budapest system, with the provincial systems often surviving on hand-me-downs from the capital. More recently tramway development in Budapest has been overshadowed by metro investment, and the provincial cities are starting to develop their own styles. The giant Ganz-Mavag industrial combine, which built many Hungarian trams, has been broken-up for privatisation.

Budapest   1866   1435mm   156 km

The Hungarian capital is a large city on the river Danube: on the west bank is the older and hilly sub-city of Buda; on the east bank the larger and newer sub-city of Pest. Many attractive buildings survive from the days of the Austro-Hungarian Empire, with old and rather dull or industrial suburbs surrounding the central area, and new housing areas further out. The extensive tramway system has been reduced in size in recent years as the modern metro has expanded, although a new line is being built to light rail standards as an outer ring in Pest. The very heavy loadings which required intensive services with three-car sets have reduced as increasing motor car ownership has followed the fall of Communism. Tatra trams were acquired to complete the replacement of older rolling stock, but efforts have been made to develop a Hungarian built articulated car for the next generation of trams. In addition to the modern metro, the shallow subway (Foldälatti) of 1896 is still in operation, with modern rolling stock. In the north-west suburb of Buda a rack tramway carries passengers to hill-top leisure areas. Suburban electric light railways run north, east and south from termini on the edge of the central area, but no longer share any trackage with the urban tramway system (there used to be through operation of goods cars). At Szentendre, the terminus of the northern line, there is a tramway and light railway museum.

Rolling stock

1301-1370	AM8	1967-71	Ganz
1400-1481	AM8	1972-8	Ganz
3200-3474	M4	1956-61	Ganz
3700-3701	M4	1948	Ganz
3750	AM6	1990	Ganz
3800-3899	M4	1962-5	Ganz
4000-4171	M4	1979-80	Tatra
4200-4349	M4	1984	Tatra
5800-5899	B2	1939	Ganz
5900-5991	B2	1951	Ganz
6000-6049	B2	1954	Ganz

Top right Two Ganz trams of the Budapest system at Kolozvar. *Karel Hoorn*

Right A more modern Tatra set in the city centre. *Westbury Marketing*

Debrecen   1911   1435mm   6 km

This provincial city in eastern Hungary has an historical city centre with green suburbs. The one-route tramway links the railway station with the northern suburbs, providing an intensive service. A standard fleet of two-rooms-and-a-bath four-axle articulated trams is to be replaced by a newly-developed medium-height floor design developed in Hungary (11 more of these trams are on order).

Rolling stock

282-290	AM4	1962	Ganz	
292-294	AM4	1962	Ganz	Ex-Budapest
381-386	AM4	1967-9	Ganz	
481-492	AM4	1969-79	Ganz	
500	AM6	1993	Ganz-Hunslet	

Right The impressive centre of Debrecen with tram 491.

Miskolc   1897   1435mm   9 km

Miskolc in north-east Hungary is an industrial city that has developed along a valley which is served by a tram route running from the railway station at the eastern end. A single-track loop serves an older housing area off the main line. A standard fleet of four-axle articulated trams has been supplemented by some Tatras bought second-hand from Slovakia

Rolling stock

100-110	AM4	1962	Ganz	
130-174	AM4	1963-78	Ganz	
200-209	AM8	1988	Tatra	Ex-Kosice

Right Two Miskolc articulated trams pass in the city centre.

Szeged   1884   1435mm   15 km

Hungary's second city is in the south-east on the river Tisza, near the Yugoslav/Romanian border. The well-preserved central area is surrounded by green suburbs and new housing areas. The tramway system declined as trolley-buses were introduced, and in addition to a cross-city street line linking railway station and city, includes other routes that are partly on reserved track. A standard fleet of four-axle articulated trams is operated.

Rolling stock

601-614	AM4	1962	Budapest	614 ex-Debrecen
651-662	AM4	1970	Budapest/Debrecen	
801-10/3-8	AM4	1972	Budapest	
812/20	AM4	1963/4	Budapest	Ex-Budapest

Right Single track with passing loops is still a feature of Szeged.

ITALY

The great cities of Milan and Turin have always been at the forefront of Italian tramway development; although Rome created the first modern articulated cars as early as 1941, the capital's system was much reduced in the 1960s and for two decades the only progress was in the north. Genoa is to be first of several new systems, but the chaotic political and economic situation of recent years has put most investment on hold. Italian manufacturers have developed new low-floor designs, and have achieved some export success.

Genoa (Genova)   1990   1435mm   3 km

The busy commercial port city on the Mediterranean coast had been without trams for many years when it was decided to build a segregated light rail line to connect a suburban bus interchange at Brin with the city centre. The first section was opened in 1990 from Brin to Dinegro through a tunnel originally built for trams, and was extended in subway to Principe railway station in 1992. Further extension to San Giorgio is under construction, and a suburban extension from Brin to Rivarolo is proposed. Tramway-type articulated cars operate in multiple unit. A rack railway runs from Principe to Granarolo, while cable tramways provide links to Righi and Santa Anna. A 25-km electric light railway runs from Genoa to Casella.

Rolling stock

01-06	AM6	1989	Firema
07-18	AM6	1992-5	Firema

The Genoa light metro uses tramway-type articulated cars.

A collection of Peter Witt trams still provides faithful service to Milan.

Milan (Milano)   1878   1445mm   205.5 km

This great commercial and industrial centre in northern Italy is a regional capital with an historic city centre surrounded by concentric ring roads. Newer suburbs have developed to the north and west, served by the metro, and to the south, served by extending the tramway. Suburban tramways run north into the city's hinterland and carry very heavy commuter traffic from towns such as Desio and Limbiate: similar lines to Cologno and Gorgonzola in the east have been replaced by metro. The city terminus of the suburban tramways is at Via Valtellina. The extensive urban tramway system reaches all parts of the city, mostly on street track though reservation on suburban dual carriageways or the middle ring is quite common. It has been decided not to build further metro lines, but concentrate on upgrading and extending the tramways to light rail standards. The new extension of route 15 south to Rozzano is the first example of this. The tram fleet still includes large numbers of Peter Witt bogie trams dating from before the war (albeit modernised several times) as well as post-war articulated trams, and a new batch of articulated cars. Orders for a fleet of low-floor trams are expected shortly.

Rolling stock

124-128	M4	1942	OM Stanga	
321-334	B4	1941	Tallero	
431-432	B4	1945	OM Stanga	Control trailers
501-512	M4	1953	Tallero	Without driving cabs
531-554	B4	1950	OM Stanga	Control trailers
801-810	M4	1941	OM Stanga	Without driving cabs
831-850	B4	1941-50	Tallero/OM Stanga	Control trailers
1503-2002	M4	1928-30	various	350 remain
4601-4613	AM6	1955	OM Stanga	
4714-4724	AM6	1957-60	OM Stanga	
4725-4733	AM6	1960	Breda	
4801-4844	AM8	1971-74	ATM/Mauri	Rebuilt from older cars
4900-4949	AM8	1976-77	Fiat	
4950-4999	AM8	1976-77	OM Stanga	

Naples (Napoli)   1875   1435mm   23 km

A port city on the Bay of Naples in southern Italy, Naples has a hilly central area with flatter areas to the east. A metro has been under construction for many years to serve the old city and northern suburbs. The tramway is a long coastal route from Bagnoli in the west to San Giovanni in the east with an inland line to Poggioreale in the north-east, but the pattern of services and the sections of route in operation vary from time to time due to road and reconstruction work. The routes are mostly in the street, with some roadside reservation, and there are two road/tram tunnels on the line to the west. There are plans to upgrade the line to light rail standards, and a section of tram subway has been built but remains disused, as do articulated trams bought to run in it. In the city centre trams run past the terminus of the Circumvesuviana railway, a light electric line running two routes east from the city. There are similar lines to the west, and several funiculars in the hilly districts.

Rolling stock

01-12	AM6	1991	Firema	Stored in subway
952-1050	M4	1934-8	Meridionali/Fiore	Rebodied 1976-82

Rome (Roma)   1882   950/1445mm   18/70 km

The Italian capital is an historic city on the river Tiber, with a crowded central area containing many fine buildings. Large suburbs have developed outside the city walls, mainly to the north, east and south and two metro lines have been built. ATAC city tramway services run around the central area, with branches to the suburban developments, and are mostly on street track. The private right-of-way near the Coliseum is attractive, while the new extension to P. Mancini is on reserved track, as is the outer end of western suburban routes. The mixed tram fleet still includes pre-war bogie trams, as well as articulated cars taken over from the suburban tramway operator ACoTraL. This undertaking still operates a narrow-gauge tramway from the south side of Roma Termini railway station to the eastern suburb of Centocelle, starting in the street, but operating for most of the way on reserved track. ACoTraL is also the operator of metro lines A and B and the standard-gauge light railways from Piramide to Ostia Lido and from P. Flaminio to Viterbo.

Rolling stock

801-803	AM8	1953	OM Stanga	ACoTraL narrow gauge
811-817	AM8	1962	Breda	ACoTraL narrow gauge
901-912	AM8	1991	Firema	ACoTraL narrow gauge
2005-2265	M4	1930-4	Carminati e Toselli	Odd numbers only
7001-7099	AM6	1948/9	OM Stanga	Odd numbers only
7101-7115	AM6	1952	OM Stanga	Ex-ACoTraL Odd numbers only
8001-8039	M4	1954/5	OM Stanga	Odd numbers only
8041/8043	M4	1958	Breda	Ex-Milan
9001-9033	AM6	1990/1	SOCIMI	Low floor

Top right Naples has rebodied its pre-war trams.

Right A pre-war Rome tram on private right-of-way by the Coliseum.

Torino (Turin)   1872   1445mm   123 km

An industrial city on the river Po, Torino is bordered by hills to the east, across the river from the historic city centre, and therefore has expanded west and south. The narrow streets in the central area accommodate tramways by gutter running and some one-way working in parallel thoroughfares, and others reserved for trams and pedestrians. In the suburbs there is some reserved track, particularly on lines upgraded to light rail standards such as routes 3 (P. Hermada – Vallette/Stadio) and 9 (Esposizione – Stampalia). Political changes have meant a stop/go policy in terms of tramway modernisation, but light rail and low-floor cars are now in service to supplement the older rebodied rolling stock, and it seems route 1 will be extended west to the town of Rivoli. Special routes operate from the Fiat works in the southern suburbs at shift-change times. There is a rack tramway from the suburb of Sassi to the Superga basilica.

Rolling stock

2800	AM6	1959	Fiat	Rebodied, low-floor prototype
2801-2857	AM6	1959/60	ATM Torino	Rebodied
3100-3224	M4	1949-57	Fiat	Rebodied
3225-3229	M4	1943	Fiat	Rebodied
3250-3279	M4	1958-9	Fiat	Rebodied
3501	M4	1948	ATM Torino	Rebodied
5001-5054	AM6	1988-9	Fiat/OM Stanga	Low-floor
5500/5501	AM6	1991/2	Firema/Fiat	Low-floor prototypes
7000-7050	AM6	1983-6	Fiat/Firema	Light rail cars

The narrow streets of Turin produce some interesting track layouts.

Trieste   1883   1000mm   5.2 km

The surviving tramway in the Adriatic seaport of Trieste is a line from Piazza Oberdan on the north side of the city centre to Villa Opicina in the hills to the north. A short section of street track from the city terminus brings the line to an incline, where the cars are pushed up by cable dummies before reaching more street track to the hilltop terminus. The line and its rolling stock have been completely modernised in recent years.

Rolling stock

401-405	M4	1935	OM Stanga
406/407	M4	1942	OM Stanga

The Opicina tram is pushed up the cable section in Trieste.

NETHERLANDS

The three large Dutch cities have all taken different development paths. Amsterdam introduced articulated trams from 1957, Den Haag was a European PCC pioneer, and later Rotterdam introduced the 'Sneltram' concept. In recent years the different strands of progress have tended to merge as the government's pro public transport policies aim towards double patronage, with new rail systems playing a key role. Belgian, Swiss and German builders have tended to supply Dutch trams, with domestic industry limited to the manufacture of electrical equipment (Holec). However future Amsterdam Sneltrams have been ordered from CAF in Spain.

Amsterdam   1875   1435mm   124 km

The historic Dutch city on the River IJ has a city centre interlaced with canals, which penetrate into older suburbs. Large new housing areas have been built to the west (served by tram), south (tram/light rail) and south-east (metro). The city has a positive public transport policy and more and more restrictions are being put on driving in the central area, where de facto tram reservations have been created by confining cars to one narrow lane. The narrow Leidsestraat has interlaced track with passing loops at canal bridges. Suburban extensions have been built on green reservations. The new line to Amstelveen in the south is served by a joint service of city trams, and light rail cars which reach the city centre over metro tracks; the cars are equipped for both pantograph 'and third-rail current collection. The light rail may be extended under the IJ to northern suburbs, while an outer ring line is already under construction. The first generation articulated trams have been partly replaced by low-floor cars. Some routes have trams with seated conductors: boarding is at the rear door only on these services. A museum tramway runs from Haarlemmermeer station to the recreation area Amsterdamse Bos at weekends from Easter to the autumn.

Rolling stock

45-57	AM6	1990	BN	Sneltram
58-69	AM6	1993/4	BN	Sneltram
602-652	AM8	1959-63	Schindler	
653-669	AM8	1964	Werkspoor	
670-724	AM8	1966-8	Werkspoor	
725-779	AM8	1974-5	LHB	
780-816	AM8	1979-80	LHB	
817-841	AM8	1990-1	BN	Low-floor
901-920	AM8	1989-90	BN	Low floor

Left The latest type of low-floor tram leaves Amsterdam's central station.

The Hague (Den Haag)   1864   1435mm   118 km

The Dutch capital is an administrative, commercial and residential city with a compact historic centre surrounded by older suburbs. Large new residential areas have been built to the south and east. The tramway system is the backbone of public transport, with some street track still in the central area, but most of the system on reservation. The interurban line south to the town of Delft is mostly on private right-of-way. Many extensions to light rail standards have been built or are planned and the east-west line through the city centre will be put in subway by 1996. An elevated tramway serves the Centraal Station, with another line at street level. Particularly attractive is the route through the woods from Madurodam to the seaside Scheveningen. The modernisation of the tram fleet has seen the traditional PCC cars replaced by a standard fleet of articulated trams. There is tram museum at the former Van Hallstraat depôt (west of Station HS) and museum cars may often be seen on the system.

Rolling stock

1317-1333	M4	1971-2	La Brugeoise	PCCs; 10 in reserve
3001-3100	AM8	1981-4	BN	
3101-3147	AM8	1992/3	BN	

Left The Hague has many kilometres of reserved track tramway.

This batch of Rotterdam articulated trams is being refurbished for further service.

Rotterdam   1879   1435mm   67 km

This major port and commercial centre on the river Maas is a modern city with expanding suburbs to the west, south and north-east. These have been served by metro construction (north-east suburbs have metro extensions built to light rail standards with overhead current collection). However the focus of transport planning has now switched back to the tramway system, which is due to be further modernised and extended. Street track is largely confined to older suburbs west and east of the city centre: elsewhere reservation is the norm. A separate tram route operates on the south bank of the river, feeding the metro at Maashaven: the eastern section of this is built to light rail standards. This line is due to be reconnected to the main system by putting trams on a new Maas bridge. Rolling stock includes some first generation articulated trams, plus modern and rebuilt cars.

Rolling stock

368-375	AM8	1965	Duewag	
606-632	AM6	1969	Werkspoor	
701-750	AM6	1982-5	Duewag	
801-850	AM6	1984-8	Duewag	Rebuilt from 1965 cars
1601-1635	AM8	1969	Werkspoor/Duewag	600-series with new centre sections

A two-car unit on the Utrecht system at IJsselstein. *Westbury Marketing*

Utrecht   1983   1435mm   18km

This commercial and industrial city in the centre of the Netherlands built large new housing areas to the south in the 1970s and a new light rail line linking these with the railway station was opened in 1983. The line is all on reserved track or private right-of-way and has high-platform stops. At the outer suburb of Nieuwegein there are branches to Achterveld and Nieuwegein Zuid. Approved plans for a new line from the railway station through the city centre and on to the eastern suburb De Uithof (to be operated by low-floor trams) have recently been postponed by a new city council.

Rolling stock

5001-5027	AM8	1983	SIG

Other lines

A heritage tramway is to be built within the Open Air Museum at Arnhem, with a museum depôt and a replica of a 1929 Arnhem tram, for completion in 1996. The traditional Dutch steam tram operation has been recreated on the museum line from Hoorn to Medemblik, operating from Easter to September.

NORWAY

Norway has always been at the fringe of tramway development, and lost the Bergen system in the 1960s. It seemed that Trondheim would go the same way, but public opinion was so pro-tram that it has supported re-opening under private enterprise. The capital city has introduced road tolls and is using the revenue for further investment in modernising and integrating the public transport rail systems. Recent trams have been built under German licence. Bergen has an operating museum tram using a short section of street track at the bus garage, operating Sundays.

Oslo   1875   1435mm   74 km

The capital of Norway is a handsome city in a beautiful situation at the head of Oslo Fjord. The centre and older suburbs give way to wooded hills all around containing many housing settlements. The tramway system has an urban network, mostly on street, but with suburban reservations such as alongside the Frogner Park. Long suburban lines on reserved track or private right-of-way run south to Ljabru and west to Jar, the latter meeting the suburban electric light railways that run from a central subway over four lines. These in turn are connected to the full metro that serves the eastern suburbs with four lines, and through running is being introduced with new and rebuilt cars. The tramway has been modernised with articulated cars, and more recently second-hand stock from Göteborg (Gothenburg). A new tramway has been built to the Akers Brygge development on the harbourfront. There is a tramway museum in the former depôt at Majorstuen.

Rolling stock

101-125	AM6	1982/3	Duewag/Strømmen	
126-140	AM6	1989/90	Duewag/Strømmen	
200	M4	1990	Tatra	
201-211	M4	1952-7	Høka	Rebuilt
212/20/33	M4	1952/3	Høka	
235-260	M4	1956-8	Høka	
266-299	M4	1958/9	Hagglund	Ex-Göteborg
551-580	B4	1955/6	Høka	
582-591	B4	1953	Hagglund	Ex-Göteborg

Trondheim   1901   1000mm   8.8 km

This small city on the Norwegian coast has a very traditional feel, with many wooden buildings, and scattered settlements on wooded hillsides. The city trams were abandoned in 1988, but in 1990 a private company was allowed to resurrect the suburban line from St Olavs gt via Munkvoll to Lian (the Graakallbanen). This operates on street in the central area, then private right-of-way into the hills to the west. Permission has now been granted for a city extension to the railway station. Articulated trams bought new by the previous operator are used. Munkvoll depôt is shared with a museum group that has a fleet of restored cars: examples are often operated over the line.

Rolling stock

90-99	AM6	1984/5	LHB

Oslo's articulated trams are built by Strømmen under Duewag licence. *B Andersen*

The Trondheim articulated trams have now been transferred to a private company.

POLAND

The standardisation of Polish tramways under Communism is disappearing as the country struggles to establish a stable free-market economy. Investment in public transport has a low priority, most development plans are on hold, and delivery of new trams from the only manufacturer (Konstal of Chorzow) has almost ceased. Further second-hand acquisitions from the west are likely.

Bydgoszcz   1880   1000mm   32 km

This expanding industrial town has a well-preserved city centre with suburban industrial and housing areas. After a period of rapid expansion 20 years ago, the tramway system has suffered from an investment hiatus because of the economic situation. The undertaking was planning conversion to standard gauge (some short lengths of mixed-gauge track were laid and some significant tramway reservations created). However this seems unlikely to occur in the current climate and now the city has trouble catching up with deferred maintenance on track and rolling stock. Modern Polish-built trams are operated; the articulated trams are not in regular service.

Rolling stock

203-222	AM6	1972-4	Konstal
223-361	M4	1977-83	Konstal

A coupled set of Konstal 105N trams on their way to the railway station in Bydgoszcz.

Czestochowa articulated trams in multiple-unit formation on poorly-maintained reserved track.

Czestochowa   1959   1435mm   10.5 km

This is now a modern industrial city, but is better-known as a centre of Catholic pilgrimage based on the small old town area. The tramway system was built new in 1959 to link housing and industrial areas, with one route, mostly on reserved track. A modern fleet of standard Polish cars is operated, including some articulated trams operated in multiple unit.

Rolling stock

618-635	AM6	1972	Konstal
636-695	M4	1976-85	Konstal

Elblag   1895   1000mm   14 km

This small town suffered badly in the war, but the city centre has been completely reconstructed, and the tramway system retained and expanded. There are three routes linking the city centre and railway stations with suburban housing areas, with a mixture of different layouts including street track, reservation, private right-of-way and single-track with passing loops.

Rolling stock

008-033	M2	1959-61	Konstal
034-061	M4	1980-6	Konstal
062-078	B2	1959-61	Konstal

Gdansk   1873   1435mm   50 km

This industrial port city on the Baltic coast, famous for its shipyards, was known as the Free City of Danzig, and suffered heavy damage during the war. More recently it was the cradle of the revolution that led to the downfall of Communism. The tramway system has been retained and modernised, with extensions to serve areas of new housing development north of the port area. Plans for further upgrading to light rail standards have been delayed by the economic situation. A standard fleet of modern Polish bogie trams is operated.

Rolling stock

101-147	M4	1975-7	Konstal	Ex-Krakow
201-418	M4	1976-86	Konstal	

Modernised two-axle trams pass the main post office in Elblag.

A tree-lined reservation on route 12 in Gdansk.

Gorzow   1899   1435mm   14 km

Gorzow is a small industrial town in western Poland, with a tramway that was threatened with bus conversion in the 1970s. However it was decided to retain electric traction, and parts of the system have been upgraded from street to reserved track. The standard fleet of Polish-built trams has been supplemented recently by the arrival of second-hand articulated cars from Kassel in Germany.

Rolling stock

71-136	M4	1976-88	Konstal	
201-208	AM4	1956	Credé	ex-Kassel
(5)	AM6	1966-7	Credé	ex-Kassel

Grudziadz   1896   1000mm   9.5 km

This small town has a two-route tramway system with an infrastructure that has changed little in the last 30 years. The two routes are single-track with passing loops and run to outer suburbs that are on the fringe of the built-up area. Rolling stock is of standard Polish bogie trams. Many of the system's own cars were destroyed in a depot fire during 1993, but the municipal council decided to retain tramway operation, and has acquired second-hand stock from other Polish undertakings, all Konstal 105N cars. The depôt has been rebuilt to its original style.

Rolling stock

37-68	M4	1982-6	Konstal	61-68 Second-hand from unknown system.

A former Kassel four-axle articulated tram in Gorzow.

The narrow streets of Grudziadz with Konstal 105N trams passing.

Katowice   1894   1435mm   245 km

Katowice is the largest town in the large industrial conurbation of Upper Silesia, and its transport undertaking provides a network of services throughout the area, serving Zabrze, Gliwice, Bytom, Chorzow, Sosnowiec and Dabrowa. The tramway system is an important part of this network, and has a range of services from dense urban operations to long interurban lines operating through semi-rural/industrial landscapes. Some sections have been upgraded to light rail standards as part of a scheme to create a regional semi-metro, but progress is slow, and in the meantime some outer sections have succumbed to bus substitution. The fleet has been the proving ground for prototype cars from Polish manufacturer Konstal in the past (the factory is in Chorzow, near Katowice), but today is standardised on articulated and bogie cars of two types. However peak-hour shuttle route 38 at Bytom still features two-axle trams.

Rolling stock

101-247	AM6	1969-73	Konstal
311-702	M4	1975-85	Konstal
954, 1118/32	M2	1950?	Konstal

Krakow   1882   1435mm   79.5 km

This ancient and beautiful city became an important industrial centre with the establishment of the nearby Nowa Huta steel works and associated new town. Today Nowa Huta is large enough to have its own internal tram routes, while other lines provide the link to the traditional city centre of Krakow, with its own suburbs. The street track here and in older suburbs is supplemented by reserved track on the interurban links and within the new town. A large fleet of articulated trams (many equipped for multiple-unit operation on the trunk routes) has been supplemented by more modern bogie cars. A batch of second-hand bogie tram sets has been acquired from Nürnberg in Germany after their proposed sale to Konya in Turkey fell through, and articulated cars are expected from Nürnberg in 1995.

Rolling stock

101-112	M4	1958	MAN	Ex-Nuremburg
201-265	AM6	1970-3	Konstal	
266-461	M4	1975-80	Konstal	
501-512	B4	1959-60	MAN	Ex-Nuremburg
701-844	M4	1981-85	Konstal	
901-904	AM6	1972	Konstal	Ex-Gorzow
905-950	AM6	1970-3	Konstal	Ex-Gdansk

Lodz   1898   1000mm   124 km

This traditional industrial city has a dense urban tramway network with interesting street track layouts arising from the narrow streets in the central area. Large new outer suburbs are often served by reserved track tramways and there are some long interurban routes extending in to the semi-rural hinterland on roadside reservation or private right-of-way. A small fleet of ex-Bielefeld articulated trams has been acquired to work the busiest of these lines. The rest of the fleet comprises standard Polish-built cars: the articulated trams have now been transferred to new companies set up to operate the interurban routes 41-46, and fleet renumbering has taken place.

Rolling stock

1-2	AM6	1970	Konstal	
384-460	M4	1977-80	Konstal	
461-499	AM6	1974	Konstal	
876-999	AM6	1972/3	Konstal	
4040-4047	AM6	1957-60	Duewag	Ex-Bielefeld

Articulated trams from Germany and Poland in service on Lodz interurban route 43.

The first design of Polish articulated tram operating in Poznan.

Shipyard cranes frame a riverfront backdrop to this two-axle set in Szczecin.

Poznan   1880   1435mm   85 km

This modern industrial city with its large new housing areas has one of the most progressive tramway undertakings in Poland, and has long wished to upgrade to light rail standards with subways in the central area, which still displays evidence of its German past. Some suburban lines have been improved, with much reserved track, but the major funding needed to deal with the whole system seems unlikely to become available in the near future. In the meantime a modern fleet of trams provides a high level of service. The Polish-built cars have been supplemented by the donation of second-hand articulated trams from Amsterdam.

Rolling stock

1-73	JM6	1970-3	Konstal	
81-331	M4	1975-90	Konstal	
851-873	AM8	1958/9	Schindler	Ex-Amsterdam

Szczecin   1879   1435mm   40 km

This important industrial city, with its shipyards on the river Oder, still shows much evidence of its German past when it was known as Stettin, although post-war reconstruction has given it a modern aspect. The tramway system expanded after the war to serve new housing areas but has remained largely static in recent years. The system is mostly in the street with some reservation on newer lines, including the cross-river route to Basen Gorniczy. The tram fleet has been modernised with standard Polish cars, but two-axle trams remain in service on three routes.

Rolling stock

213-298	M2	1956?	Konstal
331-375	B2	1956?	Konstal
601-630	AM6	1971-3	Konstal
631-1008	M4	1975-92	Konstal

Torun   1891   1000mm   11 km

The small industrial town on the river Vistula has retained and modernised its tramways, with reserved-track extensions to industrial sites, and new tracks avoiding narrow streets in the city centre. However the line to the railway station has been closed. A few articulated trams remain in peak service, but most routes are operated with standard Polish bogie cars.

Rolling stock

201-210	AM6	1974	Konstal
211-271	M4	1980-9	Konstal

Germanic architecture forms a backdrop to the trams at this junction in Torun.

Warsaw (Warszawa)   1865   1435mm

The Polish capital on the river Vistula suffered severely in the Second World War, but the historic old town has been beautifully restored. It is surrounded by a modern city centre and extensive suburbs, including both industrial areas and modern housing estates. A metro has been under construction for many years but the tramway is the backbone of the public transport system, and has been extended in recent years. Much of the system is on reserved track, including the wide thoroughfares of the central area; street track is found in older suburbs. A large fleet of standard Polish bogie trams, equipped for multiple-unit working, is operated.

Rolling stock

1-500	M4	1963-5	Konstal
528-843	M4	1966-9	Konstal
1000-1348	M4	1974-91	Konstal
2000-2005	M4	1990	Konstal

Examples of the oldest cars in service in Warsaw. *Westbury Marketing*

Wroclaw   1877   1435mm   85 km

This historic city with its well-preserved central area was known as the German city of Breslau until the end of the War. The large tramway system serves all areas of the city and has been extended into new housing estates. The system is mostly street track, with some reservation in suburban areas. Route 10 operates cross-country to Lesnica in the eastern hinterland. The tram fleet has been modernised with new Polish bogie trams.

Rolling stock

2001-2104	AM6	1970-3	Konstal	
2201-2507	M4	1975-90	Konstal	
2508- ?	M4	1977-8	Konstal	Second-hand from unknown system

Some of the newest Polish trams can be found in Wroclaw.

PORTUGAL

The Portuguese tramways have always seemed to be in a time warp, though the very high standards of former years have given way to faded elegance marred by terrible traffic problems. A slow decline will see the capital's tramway confined to a modernised coastal route with articulated trams, and some of the hilly lines with refurbished traditional cars. Porto will retain part of its riverfront tramway as a living museum.

Left Tight layouts are commonplace on Lisbon's hilly routes.

Right A Belgian-built tram passes the riverside Massarelos depôt in Porto.

Lisbon (Lisboa)   1873   900mm   80 km

The Portuguese capital is an historic city built on hills on the north shore of the Tagus river. The tramway system, once British owned, presents a historic aspect as well with much street operation, very steep gradients and about 150 traditional trams. The system is very much reduced from its peak (a metro system has been built and is being extended), and efficiency suffers from the severe traffic congestion, but the riverside route west from the city centre to Belem and Cruz Quebrada is being upgraded ready for the delivery of new low-floor trams in 1995. The two-axle trams which work the hilly routes are being modernised with new electrical equipment and rebuilt bodies. A ride on the Graca circle routes 12 and 28 is one of the wonders of the tramway world, with steep gradients, sharp curves and sections of interlaced track. Funicular tramways climb streets too steep for conventional trams.

Rolling stock

104-187	B2	1950-55	CCFL	Stored
221-281	M2	1952-63	CCFL	270 rebuilt, 44 others to follow
323-342	M4	1906	Brill	Rebodied
343-344	M4	1906	Stephenson	Rebodied
501-510	M6	1995	Duewag	Low floor
613-617	M2	1935	CCFL	
701-735	M2	1935-40	CCFL	
737-745	M2	1947	CCFL	
761-763	M2	1947	CCFL	
771-785	M2	1931	CCFL	
807-810	M4	1943	CCFL	

Porto 1870 1435mm 12 km

This attractive city on the river Douro has replaced most of its tramways with buses or trolleybuses, but retains route 18 from Boavista depot (north-west of the city centre) to the seafront at Foz (largely on reservation) until the centenary of tramways in September 1995. Recent closures have isolated Massarelos depôt, rebuilt as a splendid tram museum, but part of this riverfront line is due to be reinstated as a heritage tramway when route 18 closes. In the meantime plans are being developed for a light rail system to serve the region. Traditional trams are used in service.

Rolling stock

129-169	M2	1910-12	Brill
203-223	M2	1938-45	CCFP
270-277	M4	1926-8	CCFP
280-288	M4	1929	Familleureux

Sintra 1903 1000mm 3 km

This tourist tramway between Banzao and the coast at Praia das Macas is part of the former line that ran between Sintra railway station and the coast. It comes alive each summer running a limited service on single-track roadside reservation. Mostly only one car is used in service. Access is by the regular bus service from Sintra to Praia das Macas.

Rolling stock

1, 3, 7	M2	1903	Brill
9, 10, 12	B2	1903	Brill

ROMANIA

Seven new tramways in seven years (1984-91) were a manifestation of the electric city transport policy of the previous regime in Romania, but since the Revolution economic circumstances have made mere survival the top priority for the city undertakings. The future of the Romanian car builders is unclear, but second-hand trams from Germany started to arrive in 1994.

Arad   188?   1000mm   45.5 km

This attractive city near the Hungarian border has expanded considerably with the growth of industrial suburbs and housing areas. The tramway system has kept pace with this expansion, with many new lines, including a long interurban running east to villages in the hinterland that were once served by an electric light railway. There are nominally about 15 different tram routes. In recent years the reliability of the system has been poor with some sections served only irregularly, and rolling stock falling into bad condition. The Tatra trams have been supplemented by Romanian-built cars.

Rolling stock

1-35	M4	1984-6	Timis	Odd numbers only
2-36	B4	1984-6	Timis	Even numbers only
80-179	M4	1974-81	Tatra	
180-230	M4	1981-3	Timis	Even numbers only
181-231	B4	1981-3	Timis	Odd numbers only

Tatra trams in the broad central boulevard of Arad.

Romania's newest tramway is in Botosani, serving standard apartment blocks in this small town. *Marco Moerland*

Botosani   1991   1435mm   11 km

Romania's newest tramway is in this small town near the Ukrainian border, where construction started before the fall of Communism, and was completed in 1991 after a review of the policy of a wholesale switch to electric traction. One route links an industrial area with the railway station and town centre on street track. A small fleet of standard articulated trams provides service: a second line is under construction.

Rolling stock

1-10	AM8	1990	Bucuresti	
11-16	AM8	1987-8	Bucuresti	ex-Cluj

Braila   1900   1435mm   15 km

The small urban tramway in this industrial town on the Danube delta has been expanded by building extensions to suburban industrial sites and a second route through the central area. The system is mostly street track, with a private right-of-way across country to the southern terminus at the paper factory. The system is unusual in employing roving conductors to collect fares. A mixed fleet of Czech and Romanian-built trams is operated.

Rolling stock

19-28	M4	1978	Tatra	
29-81	M4	1979-89	Timis	31 cars
36-89	B4	1979-89	Timis	41 cars
82-91	AM8	1989	Bucuresti	

A Timis set on the town loop in Braila.

Brasov   1987   1435mm   6.7 km

The single tram route in this established industrial town links a factory with the railway station and the edge of the town centre, but is duplicated by a trolleybus route that penetrates the central area and captures most of the traffic. The route is all street track and is worked by Romanian articulated trams.

Rolling stock

1-8	AM8	1986	Bucuresti
9-12	AM6	1986	Bucuresti
13-20	AM8	1986	Bucuresti

Bucharest (Bucuresti)   1874   1435mm   155 km

The Romanian capital is a large city whose formerly elegant city centre has been much defaced by the grandiose reconstruction projects of the former regime, but many fine old buildings remain. The central area is surrounded by sprawling suburbs and industrial areas, with much new housing built in recent years. The large tramway system declined in importance as the metro system was built, and was banished from much of the city centre in favour of trolleybuses. However the largely street track system has been supplemented by new suburban extensions, many on reserved track. The undertaking imported a large fleet of Tatra trams before it started the large-scale production of articulated cars in its own workshops. Older bogie trams have been rebodied for further service. Second-hand trams from Frankfurt-am-Main and Munich started to arrive in 1994; final numbering is not yet known. The Bucharest-built eight-axle trams are to be substantially rebuilt, with new electrical equipment.

Rolling stock

001-362	AM8	1973-88	Bucuresti	
3301-3431	M4	1971-74	Tatra	
3501	AM8	1969	LHB	
4001-4049	AM6	1985/6	Bucuresti	
6001-6172	M4	1977-85	Bucuresti	Built from 1950s cars
6201-6370	B4	1977-85	Bucuresti	Built from 1950s cars

Cluj-Napoca   1987   1435mm   11.5 km

The twin towns on the Somesul river are a regional centre for local industry with many empire-era buildings in the central area. The single tram line links this with the railway station and industrial and residential suburbs, all on street track. The service has become very irregular with only a small part of the tram fleet able to be operated because of a shortage of spare parts. Random fleet renumbering makes presentation of details difficult.

Rolling stock

01-41	M4	1987	Timis	Odd numbers: some renumbered
02-42	B4	1987	Timis	Even numbers: some renumbered
107-121	AM6	1988-9	Bucuresti	some renumbered

Top right This Brasov articulated tram shows evidence of switching sections between trams.
Centre right A three-car set of rebodied trams passes a Tatra car in Bucharest.
Right The bright livery of this Cluj-Napoca tram set is matched by the driver's cab decorations.
Marco Moerland.

Evidence of poor tram and track maintenance in Constanta.

Below
The city centre of Craiova with a Timis set showing evidence of accident damage.

Constanta   1984   1435mm   42 km

This town borders the Black Sea resort of Mamaia but is a commercial port and industrial centre. The three-route tramway system was the first of a new wave of Romanian tramways built in the 1980s and links the railway station, central and industrial areas on street track. A frequent service is provided using Romanian-built articulated cars.

Rolling stock

101-175	AM8	1984-9	Bucuresti

Craiova   1987   1435mm   19 km

This industrial and university city in southern Romania has built a north-west to south-east tram route across the central area and out to industrial suburbs. There is street track in the centre and side reservation in the suburbs. A branch to the railway station is planned. Standard Romanian-built trams are operated as motor+trailer sets.

Rolling stock

001-049	M4	1987-9	Timis
001-049	B4	1987-9	Timis

A Galati Tatra tram passes a horse and cart in the old town.

Galati   1899   1435mm   35 km

This port and industrial city on the Danube delta had a metre-gauge tramway
from 1899 to 1978. In 1972 the first section of a new standard gauge system was
opened to link new housing areas with a large steelworks complex built in the
western suburbs. The standard-gauge system has expanded as the town has
grown, and as the metre-gauge lines were withdrawn. About 19 routes are operated, mostly on reservation, but many of these are limited services associated
with shift changes at the steel works. The system is reported in a poor state with
regular track and car breakdowns. An original fleet of Tatra trams has been
supplemented by Timis sets.

Rolling stock

1-50	M4	1972/3	Tatra
51-60	M4	1978	Timis
61-70	M4	1978	Tatra
71-131	M4	1980-5	Timis
301-371	M4	1978-85	Timis

Iasi   1900   1000mm   64 km

This city, a university town in north-east Romania by the Moldavian border, has expanded considerably in recent years with new housing areas surrounding the old city centre. The tramway system has changed its layout significantly as the system has expanded and there is a modern layout through much of the city. Iasi is the last Romanian system to operate two-axle trams: those that remain were rebuilt with new bodies in the last two years. The system may receive second-hand articulated trams from Mannheim in Germany.

Rolling stock

100-12	M2	1992-3	Iasi	Rebuilt from 1960s cars
100-12	B2	1992-3	Iasi	Rebuilt from 1960s cars
201-270	M4	1979-81	Tatra	
301-348	M4	1982/3	Timis	
301-348	B4	1982/3	Timis	
350	AM6	1985	Bucuresti	
351-362	AM6	1994	Bucuresti	

A rebodied two-axle set runs through high rise blocks in Iasi.

Oradea   1905   1435mm   20 km

This former Hungarian city in north-west Romania has an attractive city centre and new housing areas in western suburbs. The tramway system operates a trunk route linking the two railway stations, with railway and factory connections for some limited goods traffic, and a ring service to the north with a recent extension west, mostly street track except for the latter reservation. The system has been able to maintain a reasonable standard of service despite the economic difficulties of recent years. All trams in service are Romanian-built cars.

Rolling stock
1-13	M4	1986-9	Timis
64-100	M4	1975-85	Timis
101-113	B4	1986-9	Timis
136-172	B4	1975-85	Timis

Ploiesti   1987   1435mm   18.5 km

This town north of Bucharest is the base for the Romanian oil industry and has built a three-route tramway linking both railway stations with the town centre and industrial suburbs. The central area has street track in narrow streets. A mixed fleet of Romanian-built trams is operated.

Rolling stock
7001-7048	AM8	1987-8	Bucuresti	29 cars
7006-7049	M4	1987-8	Timis	20 cars
7106-7149	B4	1987-8	Timis	20 cars

Above Hungarian-style housing and gutter-running trams in Oradea.

Left A bright new livery on a Timis tram set in Ploiesti.

Overcrowding is common on Romanian tramways: this scene is in Resita.

Resita   1988   1435mm   9.5 km

Resita is the centre of an industrial district producing most of Romania's steel. Although the tramway was opened in 1988, a reliable service could not be provided until workshop facilities at the depot were completed in 1992. The line runs along the river valley, crossing the river and adjacent railway three times. A fleet of standard Romanian-built cars was provided, but management failures led to the suspension of service in autumn 1994. Operation resumed in February 1995.

Rolling stock

1-43	M4	1988-9	Timis	Odd numbers
2-44	B4	1988-9	Timis	Even numbers

Sibiu   1905   1000mm   10 km

This former German settlement in Transylvania has an historic and attractive city centre. A trolleybus service operates between the railway station and the central cemetery, which is the terminus of the single-track rural tramway to the village of Rasinari. The village terminus is a reversing triangle in the street, but most of the line is on roadside reservation. After a period of closure due to the poor state of the track service has resumed, and some Swiss standard trams donated by Geneva have arrived to boost the service.

Rolling stock

5-7	M4	1985	Timis	
5-6	B4	1985	Timis	
(4)	M4	1951/2	SWP	Ex-Geneva
(4)	B4	1951/2	FFA	Ex-Geneva

The village reverser at the Rasinari terminus of the Sibiu tramway.

Below A basic roadside reservation in Timisoara.

Timisoara   1899   1435mm   42 km

This attractive city is on the Banat river in western Romania close to the borders of Hungary and Serbia, and has Hungarian and German-speaking minorities. The layout of the system has changed substantially in recent years as old sections with awkward layouts have been replaced by new lines, often on reservation. There is street track in the central area. A branch to the railway station links with urban circular routes and lines to suburban housing areas. Timisoara is the site of the Timis tram-building company, and all its fleet comes from this source but second-hand trams are expected from Bremen and Karlsruhe.

Rolling stock

1-129	B4	1972-89	Timis	
130	B4	1989	Timis	Ex-Resita
230	AM6	1982	Timis	
231-359	M4	1972-89	Timis	
360	M4	1989	Timis	Ex-Resita

SLOVAKIA

The rump state of the former Czechoslovakia faces considerable economic difficulties as it tries to establish itself, and it is not clear to what extent links will be maintained with the Tatra car-building works in Prague. Proposals for an automatic mini-metro in Bratislava were abandoned for economic reasons, but may be revived with French finance, and it seems likely that tramway development will continue.

Bratislava   1895   1000mm   35.3 km

The capital of the new state of Slovakia is an attractive city on the river Danube, with a well-preserved central area. The street tramways here extend out on reservation to new housing areas in the north-west and north-east. Trams on the western route share the road tunnel under Bratislava castle. Further extensions are planned, including a possible cross-river light rail line. It is planned to convert the system to standard gauge, and some dual-gauge track is already evident. A standard fleet of Tatra cars is operated.

Rolling stock

7002-7087	AM6	1969-77	Tatra K2
7601-7612	M4	1966	Tatra T3
7701-7846	M4	1976-89	Tatra T3
7901-7946	M4	1992-3	Tatra T6

Kosice   1891   1435mm   33.6 km

This provincial town in eastern Slovakia has an attractive central area surrounded by old and new housing areas. There is street track in the central area and reservation on the new lines that have been built to serve the suburbs. A long cross-country line built in 1964 on private right-of-way runs south to the VSZ steel works, providing an intensive service at shift change times, and a tram every 20 or 30 minutes at other times. There are plans to reintroduce trams to the central precinct where they were withdrawn in 1986. After standardising on Tatra bogie trams, some new articulated cars were purchased, but 10 of these have since been sold to Miskolc in Hungary.

Rolling stock

229/298/301/302	M4	1976-9	Tatra T3
322-424	M4	1966-89	Tatra T3
500-538	AM8	1986-91	Tatra KT8
600-628	M4	1991-3	Tatra T6

Other lines

The 35-km metre-gauge TEZ electric light railway links the railway station at Poprad Tatry with the high Tatra mountain resorts of Tatranska Lomnica, Stary Smokovec and Strbske Pleso. The last section of street running was replaced in 1991 and the line is all on roadside reservation or private right-of-way. Eighteen three-section articulated cars built by Tatra provide passenger service. At Strbske Pleso there is a rack line down to the railway station at Strba.

A 5.4-km 760-mm gauge roadside interurban light railway links the railway station at Trencianska Tepla with the spa town of Trencianske Teplice. Passenger service is provided by three bogie cars and two trailers.

Left The first type
of Tatra articulated
tram in service in
Bratislava.

Below This Kosice
tram is now
reserved for private
hire duties and is in
a special livery.

Left The narrow-
gauge roadside
light railway linking
Trencianska Tepla
with its railway
station.

SPAIN

Spanish city tramways disappeared in the 1960s, apart from the residual operation in Barcelona, and the new line in Valencia is the start of a new era. Barcelona will follow, and there are also proposals for the capital, Madrid.

Barcelona   1872   1435mm   2.8 km

The Catalan capital and Mediterranean seaport has urban and suburban metro systems, but replaced its trams with buses. The surviving line links Av Tibidabo station on the FGC metro with the base station of the funicular to the Tibidabo amusement park. The tramway runs in the street and uses restored historical cars. There are plans for an urban light rail line to be built along Diagonal in the central area of Barcelona.

Rolling stock

5-10	M2	1904-15	Estrada

Sóller   1913   914mm   5 km

Sóller is a resort village on the north coast of Mallorca. An electric light railway provides the link from Palma to the old village centre, and a tramway then links the station with the beach. The line is single track with passing loops, mostly on roadside reservation, but with some street running at each end. An intensive service is provided during the summer, but there is year-round operation at reduced frequencies. The original rolling stock is still in use.

Rolling stock

1-3	M2	1913-6	Carde y Escoriaza	
4	M2	1926	Carde y Escoriaza	Ex-Bilbao
5-6	B2	1913	Carde y Escoriaza	
7	B2	1926	Carde y Escoriaza	Ex-Bilbao
8-11	B2	1913-6	Carde y Escoriaza	

València   1888   1000mm   123.8 km

In 1987 the regional rail undertaking FGV was founded to take over the electric metre-gauge light railways of the state FEVE. These linked different termini on the edge of the city centre with the hinterland towns and villages. The system has been upgraded to light rail standards and the lines to Bétera and Llíria linked by a 7-km cross-city subway opened in 1988. New rolling stock based on the Utrecht light rail vehicle was introduced. The service across the north of the city from Ademús (connecting with the cross-city line) to the coast at El Grao was closed and has been reconstructed as a reserved track tramway, re-opening to public service in summer 1994. The line north from the mid-point of the tramway to Rafelbunyol is due to be extended towards the city centre in subway and will link with a new east-west metro.

Rolling stock

1001-1005	M4	1954/5	Macosa	
1051-1055	B4	1954/5	Macosa	
3501-3506	M4	1954/5	Macosa	
3601-3610	M4	1982	Babcock y Wilcox	
3701-3730	AM6	1986-7	CAF/MTM/Macosa	
3731-3740	AM6	1990	CAF/Macosa	
3801-3821	AM6	1993/4	Duewag	Low floor
6501-6506	B4	1954/5	Macosa	
6601-6610	B4	1982	Babcock y Wilcox	Incorporate driving cab
6651-6660	B4	1982	Babcock y Wilcox	

Barcelona's Tibidabo tramway has plenty of steep gradients and sharp curves.

Soller's ex-Bilbao trams on the seafront at Puerto Soller.

Below A rebodied train set at Rafelbunol terminus on the Valencia system. *Marco Moerland*

SWEDEN

The change of the rule of the road in 1967 saw the end of Swedish street tramways, apart from the systems in Gothenburg, Malmö (since closed) and Norrköping. The first of these cities pioneered the light rail concept, and this is providing the basis for the introduction of a new line in Stockholm, where street operation has restarted in a unique commercial museum operation. Proposals for light rail in Malmö are on ice because of the economic stringency of the present national government.

Gothenburg (Göteborg)   1879   1435mm   117.6 km

Sweden's second city and major port on the river Göta has a stately central area with industrial suburbs alongside the river bank, older suburbs running inland, and many new housing areas. Traffic management ensures that traffic penetration to the city centre is minimised and the tramways are the backbone of the public transport system. The system was upgraded to light rail standards from an early date, and is 90 per cent on reserved track, including much private right-of-way fenced for high-speed operation. New extensions have kept pace with city expansion: the latest links Sahlgrenska with the main route to the south-west suburbs via a long viaduct. Route 8 to Angered is a segregated line with three-car trains and few stops to provide a fast service to a new suburb in open country: it includes several tunnels and one underground station. Trams run across the central area river bridge to the industrial area of Hisingen and suburbs beyond. Gothenburg introduced 2.65m wide trams from 1958 and built up a standard fleet of these modern cars, since supplemented with articulated trams. An active local museum group operates a summer heritage tram service over the tracks of the Gothenburg system.

Rolling stock

200	AM6	1984	ASEA
201-279	AM6	1987-91	ASEA
548-603	M4	1960-61	Hagglund
701-770	M4	1965-7	ASJ
801-860	M4	1969-72	Hagglund

Norrköping   1904   1435mm   13 km

This small town 150 km south-west of Stockholm has a compact city centre surrounded by green suburbs. The two-route tramway system was retained and modernised when Sweden changed the rule of the road in 1967, but was threatened with closure 25 years later when political changes saw plans for a new extension and new trams shelved. However the city council has decided to retain the system and carry out some upgrading. Street track in the city centre links to suburban reservations, including the most recent extension, on private right-of-way to Klockaretorpet. The trams introduced in 1967 are being supplemented by ex-Duisburg articulated cars shipped from Germany. Fleet renumbering is in progress.

Rolling stock

31-35	M4	1967	ASJ	To become 76-98
60-67	AM6	1966/7	Duewag	Ex-Duisburg (8 cars)

A Hagglund set shows old and new liveries on the Gothenburg fleet. *Karel Hoorn*

A Norrköping tram runs through a suburban housing area on street track.

A two-car set on Stockholm's Alvik-Nockeby line before conversion to one-man operation.

Stockholm   1877   1435mm   17.7 km

The Swedish capital is surrounded by the water of Lake Malaren and incorporates
several large islands. The historic old town is an island south of the modern city
centre. The sprawling suburbs, including many new housing areas, are linked by
a large metro system; two tram routes are retained as feeders to this. In the west
is the Alvik-Nockeby line 12, with its cross-platform interchange with the metro
at Alvik (requiring a scissors crossover to change from left to right-hand running
at the first stop). To the north-east the metro station at Ropsten includes the
terminus of tram 21 to the island of Lidingö. Both these lines are on private right-
of-way. In 1991 3 km of former city tram route 7 between Norrmalmstorg and the
leisure area of Djurgaarden were re-opened as a tourist and museum tramway.
Ex-Gothenburg trams provide a base service during the summer months, supplemented by the operation of historic trams at the weekends and for special occa-
sions. A completely new light rail line built to a horseshoe shape to link northern
and southern suburbs via the west has been authorised, and consideration is
being given to re-introducing further city centre tramways. There is a transport
museum at Söderhallen bus garage, open daily.

Rolling stock

301-324	M4	1944-52	ASEA	Rebuilt 1986-9
328-333	M4	1949-52	Hagglund	Ex-Gothenburg
601-613	B4	1944-52	ASJ	With driving position: rebuilt 1986-9
615-617	B4	1951-2	Hagglund	Ex-Gothenburg

Other lines

A heritage tramway is operated by the Technical Museum in Malmö during the
summer months, running on street track, and is to be extended to form a circular
line. The Swedish Tramway Museum Society, operator of the Stockholm heritage
tramway, operates the national tramway museum at Malmköping (50 km west of
Stockholm), which is open at weekends (daily during the summer school holidays).

SWITZERLAND

Although tramways in smaller Swiss cities disappeared by the 1960s, the four major cities have retained and modernised their systems, and the lakeside line in Neuchâtel has been modernised as well. Today the tramways are an essential part of an urban transport policy which is based on environmental considerations. The new light rail line serving Lausanne is the first standard-gauge Swiss tramway. Switzerland has more electric light railways than can be listed here, and some of these still have sections of street track that give them a tramway atmosphere. The Swiss manufacturers have gradually grouped, and the factories are now mostly controlled by SWP. The national museum group for trams and light railways operates the Blonay-Chamby line in the hills behind Vevey/Montreux.

The latest type of Swiss standard tram in Basel will be the last to be delivered without low floors.

Some of Basel's BLT articulated trams have been fitted with low-floor centre sections.

Basel   1895   1000mm   85.7 km

The Swiss industrial centre on the river Rhein also borders France and Germany. The compact central area is notable for its lack of motor traffic and good access by public transport, with trams on traditional street track. Street track is also prevalent in the older suburbs, but the longer suburban lines are on reserved track or private right-of-way. There is an attractive hilly and wooded private right-of-way on the circular tram route to Brüderholz and Jakobsberg. The urban tramway undertaking BVB in green livery provides service on most routes. The suburban undertaking BLT with its yellow cars runs routes 10 and 11 to Rodersdorf, Aesch and Dornach. The Rodersdorf line includes a section through French territory at Leymen, and has been improved and modernised from a suburban light railway. The outer ends of the Rodersdorf and Dornach lines are single track with passing loops. Three Rhein bridges carry trams. Modern rolling stock includes Swiss Standard cars (some dating back to the 1940s), Duewag articulated trams, and the BLT articulated trams, some with low-floor centre sections.

Rolling stock

101-115	AM6	1971-6	Schindler	BLT
201-243	AM6/8	1978-80	Schindler	BLT 231-3/6-8 low-floor centre sections
244-266	AM8	1980/1	Schindler	BLT low-floor centre sections
401-452	M4	1948-51	Schindler	
453-456	M4	1958	Schindler	
457-476	M4	1967/8	Schindler	
477-502	M4	1986/7	Schindler	
602	AM6	1962	SIG	
603-622	AM6	1967	Duewag	
623-658	AM6	1972	Duewag	
659-686	AM6	1990/1	Schindler	
1333-1344	B3	1956-64	BVB/SLM	BLT
1401-1415	B4	1947/8	FFA	
1416-1435	B4	1961/2	FFA	
1436-1475	B4	1967-9	FFA	
1476-1506	B4	1971/2	FFA	

Bern   1890   1000mm   17.6 km

The Swiss capital is an ancient city with a picturesque arcaded main street served by the tramway (and trolleybuses), which continues to bridges over the river Aare gorge. More modern commercial and suburban development has grown up around. Suburban lines are a mixture of street track and reservation, except that the recent extension to Saali is built to light rail standards on private right-of-way. Tracks from Helvetia Platz to the junction for Saali are shared with the RBS light railway, which operates tramway-type rolling stock on this line to Worb. The fleet is a mixture of Swiss standard cars and two designs of articulated tram, the last delivery being low-floor cars. There is a short funicular near the Parliament in the city centre and a longer line, the Gurtenbahn, in the suburb of Wabern.

Rolling stock

321-330	B4	1951	FFA
331-340	B4	1960/1	Schlieren
603-613	M4	1947/8	Schlieren
621-630	M4	1060/1	Schlieren
711-726	AM8	1973	Schlieren
731-742	AM8	1989/90	Vevey

The Bern design of low-floor tram was built by Vevey.

Bex   1898   1000mm   3.4 km

This short tramway is the urban section of 17 km of mainly rack light railway that connect Bex railway station with mountain resorts at Villars and Bretaye, and runs from the station through the village to the suburb of Bevieux. The line is single track with passing loops, and is laid in the street. A single tram meets all trains and operates in front of the light railway train, carrying local passengers.

Rolling stock

15/16	M3	1948	Schlieren

The Bex tram on its way from village to railway station.

Geneva (Genève)   1862   1000mm   9.6 km

This French-speaking city at the end of Lac Léman is an international commercial centre surrounded on three sides by French territory. Busy tram route 12 runs from the French border at Moillesulaz in the east through the city centre and south to a new extension to a suburban park-and-ride point at Bachet. The line is mostly street track (sometimes serving traffic-free streets), though the new extension is on reservation. A new route 13 has been built, branching from route 12 at Plainpalais and running to the railway station. A fleet of low-floor trams has been purchased and multiple-unit operation of two cars is normal. Some cars will be extended by the addition of new centre sections. Lausanne-type LRVs operate the suburban rail service from Genève Cornavin to La Plaine.

Rolling stock

801	AM6	1984	Vevey
802-845	AM6	1987-9	Vevey

Above Geneva was the first Swiss tramway system to adopt the low-floor tram.
Below The Lausanne light rail line is single track with passing loops.

Lausanne   1991   1435mm   7.8 km

The lakeside city of Lausanne has a hilly central area and sprawling suburbs, served largely by trolleybuses. Rack tramways connect the railway station with the upper town (Flon) and the lakeside (Ouchy). A new light rail line was opened in 1991, running from an enclosed but street-level terminus at Flon west to the University and Renens suburban railway station. The line is single track with passing loops (some are being extended to permit a reduced headway), and is mostly on surface reservation alongside roads, with high-platform stations at stops. The articulated cars have a diesel motor for manoeuvring on non-electrified tracks at the depôt. There is a rail connection at Renens, and dual-system through operation on CFF tracks is a future possibility. Five more cars are on order.

Rolling stock

201-212	AM6	1990	Vevey

Neuchâtel   1892   1000mm   8.8 km

The town of Neuchâtel rises up on the north shore of the lake of the same name, and its urban tram routes have been replaced mainly with trolleybuses. An upgraded tramway runs on reservation from the lakeside in the town centre at Place Pury to the villages of Areuse and Boudry to the west. The line is single track with passing loops and features high-speed operation. A modern fleet of motors and control trailers can operate up to four-car trains.

Rolling stock

501-504	M4	1981	Schlieren
505/506	M4	1988	Schindler
551-554	B4	1981	Schlieren

The lakeside tramway between Neuchâtel and Boudry.

A Zürich museum tram meets an articulated set on street track.

Zürich   1882   1000mm   68.5 km

This is the largest city in Switzerland and its most important commercial centre, with some industrial suburbs. The city rises on a series of hills from Lake Zürich. The large tramway system is mostly on street track (including traffic-free streets in the city centre), but central control and traffic management priorities for public transport permit an efficient operation. Some suburban sections are on reservation and a major new line has been built to Schwamendingen in the north-east using in part a subway built for a metro project that never received full authorisation. Route 6 to the hilltop Zoo is an attractive line. Tracks from Stadelhofen station east of the city centre to the suburb of Rehalp are shared with the Forchbahn light railway that operates tramway-type rolling stock on its 16.6 km line to Forch and Esslingen. The Zürich tram fleet is based on Swiss Standard trams and articulated cars, including some without driving cabs that run as the second car in two-car sets. There is a short cable funicular to the Poly in the city centre and a longer automatic line up to the Rigiviertel, while a rack line runs from Romerhof up the Dolder hill. Museum trams are kept at the former Wartau depôt and provide public trips on some summer Saturdays.

Rolling stock

719-770	B4	1946-53	SIG	
771-798	B4	1959-63	SIG/FFA	
799-801	B4	1973	FFA	
1379-1415	M4	1947-54	Schlieren	
1416-1430	M4	1959/60	Schlieren	
1601-1726	AM6	1966-69	Schlieren/SIG	1691-1726 without driving cabs
1801	AM6	1961	SIG	
1802	AM6	1960	Schlieren	
2001-2045	AM6	1976-8	Schlieren	
2046-2098	AM6	1985-7	SWP	
2099-2121	AM6	1991/2	SWP	
2301-2315	AM6	1978	Schlieren	Without driving cabs
2401-2420	M4	1985-7	SWP	Without driving cabs
2421-2435	M4	1992	SWP	Without driving cabs

Other lines

Swiss electric light railways with tramway characteristics include the following:

RBS - Bern to Worb (1000mm);

BTI - Biel to Täuffelen and Ins (1000mm);

BD - Dietikon to Bremgarten and Wohlen (1000mm);

FB - Zürich to Forch and Esslingen (1000mm);

FLP - Lugano to Ponte Tresa (1000mm);

FART - Locarno to Domodossola (1000mm);

FW - Frauenfeld to Wil (1000mm);

NStCM - Nyon to La Cure (1000mm);

TB - St Gallen to Trogen (1000mm);

WB - Liestal to Waldenburg (750mm);

WSB - Aarau to Schöftland and Menziken (1000mm)

However the classification of Swiss lines raises passions with many railfans, so the above must be regarded as the author's choice!

TURKEY

Until recently Turkey was a country without tramways, the once-great Istanbul system having disappeared in the 1960s. Now there are light rail proposals for several cities. Only Istanbul is in Europe. A tramway operates in Konya in the Asian part of Turkey.

Istanbul   1989   1435mm   15.6 km

The great Turkish city that spans the Bosphorus opened a new light rail line in 1989 to link Aksaray on the western edge of the old city on the European side with large suburban bus interchange at Esenler. This segregated, high-platform line is being extended south-west to serve the airport. Rolling stock consists of three-car trains of Swedish-built articulated cars. In 1992 a street tramway was built to link Sirkeci station on the Golden Horn with Aksaray, and has since been extended west to Topkapi bus station. Pending the delivery of new low-floor trams, some of the light rail cars were fitted with skirts to operate on the tramway (which has platforms built in the street to match the high floor cars). There is also a restored tramway with museum cars operating between Taksim and Tunel along a pedestrianised street in the new town.

Rolling stock

101-135	M4	1988/9	ASEA	No driving positions
501-570	M4	1988/9	ASEA	22 adapted for street operation

The temporary terminus of the Istanbul light rail line at Esenler.

Museum trams operate through the streets of Istanbul.

YUGOSLAVIA

The present Yugoslavia comprises the states of Serbia and Montenegro, with only the capital of the former having a tramway system.

Belgrade (Beograd)   1880s   1000mm   60 km

The capital of the former Yugoslavia is an historic city at the confluence of the Danube and Sava rivers, but there are relatively few old buildings in the modern city centre and much new housing in the expanding suburbs. The tramway system has six lines radiating from a central area circular route. There is traditional street track, but much reservation on newer routes to the south and west. The newest route crosses the Sava river to serve new housing developments. After a period of very mixed and interesting rolling stock, Tatra trams from Czechoslovakia have been used to create a modern fleet. The economic sanctions of 1993-4 have had an effect on the ability of the undertaking to maintain services.

Rolling stock

101-114	M4	1973-74	Duro Dakovic
201-390	AM4	1980-89	Tatra

A Duro Dakovic tram set on gutter track in Belgrade.

UNITED KINGDOM

After 30 years with Blackpool as Britain's only tramway, the last decade has seen a resurgence of interest in this form of transport, and the return of trams to the streets of Manchester and Sheffield. However progress continues to be hampered by the financial stringency of the government. It is ironic that France's newest trams (for Strasbourg) are being built in England, while the new British systems have imported their cars from continental manufacturers.

Blackpool   1885   1435mm   18 km

Britain's first electric tramway, opened in 1885, survived to become the last street tramway in the country before the construction of new systems in recent years. It runs the length of the seafront promenade, mostly on reserved track, but with a short section of street track. The tramway extends north of the Borough boundary to serve Thornton Cleveleys and the nearby market town and port of Fleetwood. Some sections of this line are on private right-of-way: there is street track in Fleetwood. The Blackpool tram fleet was substantially renewed in the 1930s, and much stock from that era survives, including double-deck trams, although many have been rebuilt. Motor trams of the 1950s have been scrapped. Trailers of the 1960s survive, and a small number of modern trams were delivered in the 1980s.

Rolling stock

5-11	M4	1972-5	Blackpool	Rebuilt from 1934 cars
602-607	M4	1934	English Electric	Open "boat" cars
619	M4	1987	Bolton Trams	Crossbench car rebuilt from 1934 car
621-637	M4	1937	Brush	
641-648	M4	1984-88	East Lancs/Blackpool	
671-680	M4	1958-62	Blackpool	Rebuilt from 1935 cars
681-687	B4	1960/1	Metro-Cammell	With driving cabs
700-726	M4	1934/5	English Electric	Double-deck
761/2	M4	1979/82	Blackpool	Rebuilt from 1934/5 cars
732-736	M4	1961-5	Blackpool	Illuminated trams, rebuilt from older cars

This Blackpool Brush-built tram carries traditional livery.

London   1987   1435mm   21.3 km

The disused Docklands area east of the City of London has been redeveloped as a residential, business and financial area and the Docklands Light Railway was built to support this regeneration. Automatic train operation was selected for the system, which is therefore completely segregated, partly on or alongside existing or former rail alignments and partly on new viaduct, and can therefore use third rail current collection. An underground section provides a link to Bank in the City. A new line through the former Royal Docks to Beckton was opened in 1994, initially as a self-contained service to Poplar interchange station because a different ATO system is used. The initial fleet of 11 German-built articulated cars is in the process of being sold to Essen in Germany, and the expanded system is operated by similar cars built in the UK and Belgium. The DLR is now owned and operated by the London Docklands Development Corporation, but is integrated with the London Transport fares system. There are plans for an extension under the River Thames from the Isle of Dogs to Greenwich and Lewisham.

Rolling stock

01-11	AM6	1986/7	LHB
12-21	AM6	1989/90	BREL
22-91	AM6	1991-3	BN

Much of the Docklands Light Rail system is on elevated track. A train approaches Prince Regent.
Capital Transport

Manchester   1992   1435mm   32 km

This industrial and commercial city had three main railway stations on the edge of the central area. The Manchester Metrolink light rail scheme promoted by the Greater Manchester Passenger Transport Executive was designed to take over two existing rail lines (Bury - Manchester Victoria and Altrincham - Manchester Deansgate) and link them by new construction, including street track through the city centre and a branch to Manchester Piccadilly, which terminates in the under-croft of the rail station. The high platforms of the former rail stations have been retained, and the street stops have been built with short high-platform sections, while the cars have retractable steps at the entrance doors. The articulated cars, which can run in multiple-unit, were built in Italy. There are plans to build branches from the Altrincham line to Salford Quays and Dumplington, and to take over the rail line to Oldham and Rochdale for Metrolink operation, while new street-based lines may run to eastern Manchester and south to the Airport.

Rolling stock

1001-1026	AM6	1991/2	Firema

Piccadilly Gardens station on Manchester Metrolink. *Capital Transport*

Newcastle   1980   1435mm   59.5 km

This industrial city is a regional centre for the Tyneside conurbation, including Gateshead, South Shields and Tynemouth. The Tyne & Wear Metro was built as the key to an integrated passenger transport system, taking over run-down urban railways and linking them by new tunnels under Newcastle and Gateshead, with a new bridge across the river Tyne between the two. Although completely segregated, and electrified at 1500 V dc, the metro is a manually-driven system built on light rail principles. A new extension to Newcastle Airport was opened in 1991 and there are plans to extend the system to Sunderland on Wearside. The articulated cars, which operate in multiple unit, were built in Britain using a licence for the German Stadtbahn-B design.

Rolling stock

4001-4002	AM6	1976	Metro-Cammell
4003-4090	AM6	1978-81	Metro-Cammell

A Tyne & Wear Metro unit at Pelaw. *Colin Stannard*

Sheffield   1994   1435mm   30.5 km

The hilly and industrial city of Sheffield has a modern city centre and is busy promoting the regeneration of the Don Valley industrial area where the traditional steel industry has largely disappeared. South Yorkshire Supertram is a three-line system promoted by the Passenger Transport Executive, approved in December 1990 and opening in 1994-5 to link the city centre with residential areas and the Don Valley. Whilst most of the system is street-based, with reservation where possible, the Don Valley line is on private right-of-way, partly on or alongside older railway alignments. It runs to the giant Meadowhall retail centre to the north, and was opened for public use in March 1994. The second line to open runs south and east to Gleadless and Halfway, the third line north-west to Hillsborough and Malin Bridge, both opening in stages during 1995. The German-built three-section articulated trams have low floors in the outer sections to match stop platform heights at the doorways, and interior steps to high-floor sections above the powered bogies. All bogies must be powered to cope with the gradients of up to 10 per cent on the system. The scope for extending the Don Valley line to the nearby town of Rotherham is being investigated.

Rolling stock

01-25	AM8	1993/4	Duewag

South Yorkshire Supertram 13 crosses the highway under traffic signal control at Crystal Peaks en route to Halfway. *M R Taplin*

Other lines

Proposals are being prepared for new tramway systems in the West Midlands (Birmingham), Leeds, south London (Croydon), Nottingham, Bristol, South Hampshire (Portsmouth-Fareham) and Glasgow. In late 1994 the Government announced it was willing to provide funding for Midland Metro and Croydon Tramlink, subject to significant private sector involvement.

A horse tramway is operated during the summer months along the Promenade at Douglas, Isle of Man. This connects at its north end with the Manx Electric Railway, an electric light railway running along the coast to Laxey and Douglas. At Laxey there is an electrified mountain railway to the summit of Snaefell, another summer-only operation. At Llandudno in North Wales there is a cable tramway to the summit of the Great Orme which includes some street running on its lower section. At Crich in Derbyshire the National Tramway Museum operates a collection of restored trams from many systems. Other heritage tramways are found at Carlton Colville (near Lowestoft), the Black Country Museum at Dudley in the West Midlands, at Heaton Park in Manchester, and at the North East Museum at Beamish in County Durham. At Seaton in South Devon a miniature electric tramway connects the resort with the villages of Colyford and Colyton, using small-scale replicas of British tramcar designs.

DENMARK, IRELAND, GREECE, LUXEMBOURG, SLOVENIA

At present there are no tramway systems in these countries, though the capital cities København (Copenhagen), Dublin and Athenai (Athens) all have plans for light rail systems at an advanced stage of preparation. The Danish Tramway Museum Society have an operating museum at Skjoldenaesholm, 30 km west of København. There is a small tram museum operation at Hollerich bus garage in Luxembourg.

FURTHER READING

Tramway & Light Railway Atlas - Germany 1992 (Blickpunkt Strassenbahn). *
Strassenbahn Atlas Schweiz 1993 (Blickpunkt Strassenbahn). *
Tramways & Light Railways of Austria, Hungary and Yugoslavia 1988 (Blickpunkt Strassenbahn).
Tram Tours of Lisbon by Joseph Abdo (Represse). *
Light Rail Review 3-6 by Fox and Taplin (Platform 5/LRTA). *
Light Rail & Modern Tramway - monthly (LRTA/Ian Allan)
World Gazetteer of Tram, Trolleybus and Rapid Transit Systems by R. Peschkes (Rapid Transit Publications) †
Blickpunkt Strassenbahn - bi-monthly (Blickpunkt Strassenbahn eV, D) †
Der Stadtverkehr - monthly (EK-Verlag, D) †
Op de Rail - monthly (NVBS, NL) †
Tram 2000 - monthly (Tram 2000 asbl, B) †
Tram - bi-monthly (Leutweiler Verlag, CH) †
Eisenbahn - monthly (Minirex Verlag, A) †
Chemins de Fer Regionaux et Urbains - bi-monthly (FACS, F) †

* Available from LRTA Publications, 13A The Precinct, Broxbourne, EN10 7HY
† Available from RTP, 37 Wellesley Rd, Ilford, IG1 4JX